HAUNTED
HASTINGS

HAUNTED
HASTINGS

TINA BROWN

Frontispiece: *There are secret caves and tunnels, a legacy of the town's smuggling past, all over Hastings, and many of them are haunted.*

First published in 2006 by Tempus Publishing
Reprinted 2007

Reprinted in 2010 by
The History Press
The Mill, Brimscombe Port,
Stroud, Gloucestershire, GL5 2QG
www.thehistorypress.co.uk

British Library Cataloguing in Publication Data.
A catalogue record for this book is available from the British Library.

ISBN   978 07524 3827 6

Typesetting and origination by
Tempus Publishing Limited.
Printed in Great Britain.

CONTENTS

Acknowledgements   6

Introduction   7

1   Hastings Old Town   11

2   Central Hastings   57

3   St Leonards   67

4   West St Leonards to Bexhill   85

5   Surrounding Villages   91

ACKNOWLEDGEMENTS

A huge thank you to all those who have contributed and helped with this book – including the ghosts, without you it would not have been possible.

This book is for those special people in my life – wherever in the world you are – writing makes everyone seem a little bit closer.

INTRODUCTION

The Hastings area – encompassing Hastings Old Town, Burton St Leonards, West St Leonards, Bexhill and the surrounding villages – has a rich history. The area offers vibrant contrasts, from the quaint streets and passageways of Hastings Old Town to the elegant resort of Bexhill, and each area is unique in its character, architecture and atmosphere. There have been many visitors to this part of the country over the centuries; many have chosen to stay. The past lingers here and many people have caught glimpses of the unknown.

I have always had a fascination with ghosts, witches and 'things that go bump in the night'. I remember how, as a child, I longed to go on ghost hunts and visit haunted houses but had to make do with historical guidebooks and my creative mind to make up my own spooky tales! In 1993 I became involved in events for Old Town Week. This annual festival, with walks, talks, music, street parties and a carnival, is the highlight of the year for visitors and locals alike. I suggested holding a ghost walk around Hastings Old Town, touring the haunted houses and pubs, and the idea was well received. I didn't have long to organise it and for the following two months I did nothing but eat, sleep and breathe ghosts. Every free second I had, I was researching something else and I loved every minute of it, from going to dinner at a haunted house to interviewing locals about their ghostly encounters. At that time, I worked in the Old Town and local residents would pop into the office every day, either to bring me new snippets of information and possible hauntings or just to see how I was doing – the support was tremendous and still continues today. In a little over eight weeks, I had researched the history and spooky happenings of the Old Town and, thanks to the local people and the media, I was able to create something unique to the Old Town to add to the week of activities.

I didn't know just how popular the subject of ghosts was until the first night of the ghost walk. I had anticipated a handful of family and friends; I was not prepared for around 100 people to turn up! I had no experience of being a guide, and to say I was a nervous wreck was an understatement. Thirteen years later, I am still involved in the Old Town Week events and I have become an accepted sight wandering round the Old Town like the Pied Piper with groups trailing behind me, hoping for a glimpse of a ghost.

Every year, I am told new stories and information to add to my collection. I am always meeting more interesting characters eager to pour out their tales of the dark side and their own spooky encounters and since 1993 I have met some fantastic people. I have been involved with raising money for local charities, I appeared on Channel 4's *The Salon* being given a spooky hairdo, and I have taken a group of employees from Disney headquarters on a tour. In more recent years I have extended my investigations and gathered together numerous intriguing tales from the modern part of Hastings, as well as from St Leonards, West St Leonards and the surrounding villages.

I have put together an enchanting ensemble of tales to mystify and terrify those who choose to believe. Please join me on an exploration of where the past meets modern life and where mysticism and folklore linger on. Let us discover the ancient secrets that would otherwise go untold.

Tina Brown
January 2006

Above and opposite: *People have been drawn to the Hastings area for centuries. The town has a rich history and hides some ancient secrets.*

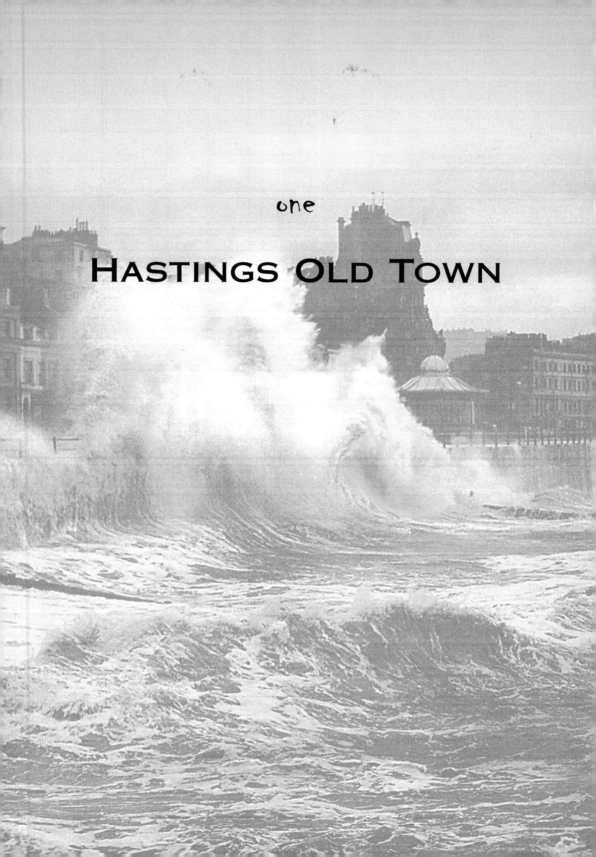

one

HASTINGS OLD TOWN

The Stag Inn

This inn in All Saints Street dates back to the sixteenth century and is a real delight. It houses a collection of mummified cats and rats which were found in the fireplace when some work was being done. The animals are said to have been put there in the 1500s by the black witches of Hastings, to ward off evil spirits. They are displayed in a glass cabinet in the front of the inn – have a look, if you dare.

The Stag inn has connections with smugglers. In the 1950s, a secret passageway was found leading from the inn, down through the sandstone cliffs, to the beach on Rock-a-Nore. Gold coins and kegs of brandy dating back to the height of the smuggling period were discovered in the passageway, left by the smugglers in their haste to avoid capture and certain death at the hand of the customs men.

The inn has its very own ghost, the captain of a ship which was set upon by the most evil band of smugglers in Hastings, the Chopback smugglers. They got their name from their method of murdering their victims: chopping them on the back of the neck and back with an axe. First, they would lure a ship into the harbour with a false light, then they would creep aboard the ship and brutally murder everyone to make sure that no one on board could identify them. They would then gather together all the ship's cargo – perhaps gold, lace or sugar – and bring it ashore to Hastings. The captain who haunts the Stag Inn was one of the Chopbacks' unfortunate victims. Many people have seen him around Christmas and they all describe him as a tall regal-looking gentleman, wearing deep purple velvet robes and a large hat with a huge feather and jewels in it. If anyone speaks to him or approaches him, he simply walks through the fireplace, which is the entrance to the secret passageway through the caves. It is said that the captain has come back to seek his revenge on descendants of the Chopback smugglers who live in the Old Town today.

A fascinating sight can be seen in the back bar area of the Stag inn: two mysterious black marks, resembling footprints, on the floor by the door. No one knows how they got there and they are known as witches' footsteps. Over the years, attempts have been made to get rid of them by sanding the floor and even by replacing the wooden floorboards but, as if by magic, the marks always reappear.

The Stag inn in All Saints Street is a place of secret passageways, ghostly captains and mummified animals.

The Lookout Point

Passageways from All Saints Street lead up the East Hill, where the Lookout Point on the edge of the cliff gives breathtaking views of the town and the sea. It is possible to see Hastings Pier and, directly below, the area known as The Stade (a Norman word meaning landing place). On a fine day, you can see all the way to Eastbourne and Beachy Head.

The Lookout Point is haunted by the grandmother of a fishing family who suffered a tragic loss in 1701. The whole family were involved in the fishing industry, with the sons following their fathers to sea and the women selling the fish in the market. During one of the worst storms seen in Hastings, all the men of the family drowned, a loss felt by the whole community. It is said that the grandmother came to the Lookout Point on the evening of the storm, watching and waiting for her menfolk as she had done so many times before. She never saw any of them again.

The grandmother has been seen at the Lookout Point, dressed in long skirts, a shawl and boots, with her hair blowing in the wind, and the sound of crying has been heard. It is said that she will haunt this place until she is reunited with her family. Many people have seen the mysterious figure but it disappears by the time they reach the Lookout Point from the East Hill or from one of the nearby cottages.

Above and below: *All Saints Street.*

An eighteenth-century woman has been seen at Lookout Point, watching for a fishing boat that was lost at sea.

Many boats have been lost in stormy weather over the years.

This was once the butcher's shop where the notorious Sweeney Todd worked in the eighteenth century.

Sweeney Todd

Today, No. 32 High Street houses a very elegant bridal shop but it has a dark and murky past due to its association with the infamous Sweeney Todd. In 1760 the shop was Harris the butchers. It was popular with Old Town folk and Harris pies and sausages were legendary throughout the south of England. Sweeney Todd, who was born in Newgate in London in 1748, came to Hastings at the age of fourteen to get away from the dirt of London and to find some work. It was not long before the young chap was snapped up by Mr Harris the butcher and taken on as his apprentice. Mr Harris was delighted at having found such a keen and eager young chap to train in his trade.

Sweeney Todd was pleased to find such a position and thought himself doubly lucky because Mr Harris had a young and beautiful daughter, whom Sweeney Todd planned to marry. After six months of employment, Sweeney plucked up the courage to propose to Miss Harris – but she turned him down. Sweeney had not expected a refusal and it changed his personality. He felt a terrible desire to slit Miss Harris's throat so that she could not tell anyone about his proposal.

The Stables Theatre is haunted by the Pretty Ghost, who will glide across the stage on opening night if the show is going to be a success.

One night, Sweeney Todd crept into the upstairs room of the butcher's shop and found Miss Harris doing some paperwork. She was all alone as her father had gone out for the evening. Sweeney took his chance and with one stroke of the knife, she was dead. He dragged her body downstairs, cut it up and, it is said, made it into sausages and pies to sell in the shop.

Sweeney Todd left Hastings in 1762 and returned to London, where he was caught pickpocketing and sent to Newgate Gaol until he was nineteen. After his release, he set up a barber's shop in Fleet Street – and the rest is history...

The Pretty Ghost

At the top of the High Street can be found the Stables Theatre and Art Gallery. In 1956, stable blocks used by troops in Napoleonic times faced demolition until the Old Hastings Preservation

The young girl threw herself to her death from the cliffs at Fairlight.

Society saved the building, lovingly restoring it and converting it into the impressive theatre and art gallery we have today. During the work on the building, the OHPS saved as many of the original bricks as possible and extensive restoration work has been carried out over the years. Inside, many of the original beams are still visible. The theatre was opened by Sir Ralph Richardson in 1959 and since then the Stables Theatre Guild has presented many productions. The art gallery is also very successful, exhibiting many famous artists.

In keeping with the beautiful building, the theatre has an elegant ghost. Known as the Pretty Ghost, she is said to be the daughter of a well-to-do family who lived in Hastings Old Town during the Napoleonic wars. She fell very much in love with one of the soldiers who kept his horses at the stables. The couple would go for long, romantic walks over the East Hill to Fairlight and plans were made for them to marry when the war ended. Tragically, the young soldier was sent away to battle and was killed in action, never to return to his fiancée. On hearing of her sweetheart's death, the girl was distraught and threw herself to her death from the cliffs at Fairlight where they had spent so much time together.

The Pretty Ghost haunts the theatre which was the tragic couple's meeting place. There have been numerous reported sightings over the years and they have all described a similar figure, that

Number 13 Croft Road (the middle cottage), where the figure of an old lady has been seen on the stairs.

of a young, tall and elegant lady who is impeccably dressed. This is a ghost that people actually want to see, as the story goes that the Pretty Ghost will glide across the stage of the theatre on the opening night of a production if the show is going to be a success.

The Friendly Ghost at No. 13 Croft Road

Walking down Croft Road, in the Old Town, feels like being back in another century, with its small black and white cottages. Number 13 was built in the late fifteenth century and many of the beams used in the construction of the cottage came from shipwrecks on the Old Town beach. The house is said to be haunted by a benevolent Edwardian ghost and, on entering, a tranquil atmosphere can immediately be felt. The figure of an old lady has been seen gently

19

Walking around Croft Road and Hill Street feels like being back in another century and it is easy to imagine ghosts round every corner.

rising up the tiny, twisting staircase and disappearing into one of the upstairs rooms. The lady is reported to be small in stature, wearing a long, dark dress and with her hair neatly tied up in a bun. Before she appears, the heady fragrance of lavender pervades the house and the rustle of taffeta is heard; lavender was a popular fragrance during Edwardian times and ladies' gowns were often made of taffeta. Whoever sees the ghost experiences a feeling of complete calm and no one has ever felt any fear; on the contrary, the old lady is a very welcome and much-loved ghost.

This friendly ghost is said to be the great-grandmother of the family who lived at No. 13 Croft Road in the Edwardian era. At that time, Hastings was a very popular place to come for holidays. Visitors would travel from London to breathe the fresh sea air, which was particularly beneficial to people with respiratory problems. They would often stay for several months and some people, after discovering the delights of the Old Town, never went back to their old lives in the city and instead stayed here for the rest of their lives. The great-grandmother was one such visitor: she spent a happy month or so in Croft Road, enjoying the sea air and relaxing. Legend says that she enjoyed her time in the Old Town so much that she never went home and her ghost lives on in the cottage today.

St Clement's church was built around 1380. There are two round objects set in the stones high on the belfry wall – it is said that one is a cannonball fired during an invasion and the other was put there by locals to even up the effect!

The Lord Nelson

Staff and regulars at the Lord Nelson inn have often seen the ghost of Joseph Swaine, a young fisherman in the nineteenth century. The Old Town fishing community has always been a very close and supportive community, caring for one another and preserving their rich heritage and history, while at the same time providing the Old Town with quality catches of fresh fish, which are loved by many. This ancient trade goes back centuries and is really the backbone of the Hastings that we know today. The fishermen are right to be proud of their unique fleet of fishing vessels and their net huts; the black sheds built on the beach. These tall structures provided airing space for the fishing nets and ropes and also storage for fishing equipment and many have been preserved. The old fishing quarter would have been found along All Saints Street and the bottom end of The Bourne, with tiny cottages housing the fishermen and their families. These were very poor people, many of them living with several family members in small rooms. The sons of the families were expected to follow their fathers into fishing, as this was the tradition. The Swaines were one such fishing family and Joseph Swaine, who lived in a tiny cottage at the bottom of All Saints Street with his family, was well known and well liked in the community. In 1812 Joseph was killed by a customs guard and his death was a terrible loss to the fishing community.

This ghost of Joseph Swaine is often seen in the Lord Nelson; his presence is accompanied by severe drops in temperature and strange smells.

Fishing provided a cover for smugglers coming into the harbour; many poor fishermen were asked to bring in goods in their fishing boats and were offered money to do so. Smugglers often disguised their boats as fishing vessels and dressed as fishermen to fool the customs guards. This worked quite well until the customs guards realised that they were being made fools of and brought in a new rule: anyone caught impersonating a fisherman and smuggling goods would be instantly shot. This still did not deter all of the smugglers, as they were very crafty and clever in their operations and the thought of the money they would get for their illicit goods was too tempting. On the night that he was killed, Joseph Swaine had been out to sea off the beach in Hastings Old Town. As he returned to the shore, the customs guards assumed he was a smuggler and shot him dead. Not long after this tragic event, the customs guards were stripped of the authority to shoot suspected smugglers, as the government realised that the Hastings fishermen were far too valuable to risk losing any more at the hands of the customs guards.

Joseph's ghost lingers near the street where he was born and spent all his life. He even has a passageway named after him; it lies off All Saints Street and leads up to Tackleway. The Lord Nelson stands at the southern end of The Bourne and is very near to the place where Joseph was shot dead. He has been seen in the inn on numerous occasions and has been described as a young, slightly scruffy-looking chap wearing a fishing tunic and a strange-shaped hat. There have been reports of him walking through the back wall of the inn as if going to All Saints Street or Rock-a-Nore Road. He has been spotted by regulars at the inn and by people who have worked there over the years; some say that he has come back to check up on his fishermen descendants. Whenever he is seen, there is an accompanying severe drop in temperature and also a very strange smell that no one has been able to identify.

The Old Post Office

Halfway up the High Street is the old post office, a building which held a dark secret for many years. The post office was once the heart of the community and people used it as a meeting point; all that now remains to remind us of the building's previous function is the red Royal Mail collection box set into the outside wall. The building, which had lain empty for decades, was saved from ruin in the 1960s and extensive reconstruction work was carried out on the interior rooms. However, the workmen found more than just spiders hiding in the upstairs rooms – they uncovered a secret which had been locked away and was never expected to be found.

In the mid-nineteenth century, the shop was owned by the Farrow family. The two sons, Samuel and Timothy, ran the family coffin-making business. They were skilled in the craft of coffin-making and took great care over each piece that they made. The Farrows were well known and respected in the Old Town community, however, Samuel and Timothy's mutual hatred was also well known in the area. Even as young children they never got on and as they got older the intense dislike continued to grow, although when they became responsible for the family business, they had to find a way of working together.

One day, the brothers were seen fighting in the High Street outside their business. Onlookers feared for Samuel's life because Timothy was giving him a severe beating. They witnessed

The old post office was once a coffin-maker's and hid a tale of fraternal hatred.

Samuel being knocked to the ground and then being dragged up the staircase to the side of the shopfront, into the upstairs rooms. No one ever knew what caused the argument but it was the worst fight that anyone had ever seen; little did they know that they would never witness another fight between the two brothers again.

Local residents became worried about Samuel when he was no longer seen around the community. However, when they enquired about his whereabouts they were told that he had decided that he could not work with Timothy any more and so had moved away to family in the country. No one thought any more about it. The years went by and Timothy eventually died of old age at the age of ninety-four. It is said that he carried on making coffins until his dying day; when his body was found, he had been working on his own coffin.

For years after Timothy's death, the building stood empty. No one ventured near the place as it had an eerie atmosphere and some people felt that they were being watched as they walked past. It was badly neglected until the 1960s, when work began to turn it back into the attractive building it had once been. No one had been inside since the day Timothy was carried out in his coffin and there was a great deal of work to do in clearing old wood and materials from the upstairs rooms. There were also many coffins standing in one corner of the workshop; these were lifted and carried down the stairs.

When one of the builders lifted up a coffin, he felt something move inside. Intrigued, he removed the coffin lid – which had been nailed down although none of the others had sealed lids. Inside was a skeleton in a hunched-up position with the hands pressed against the inside of the coffin lid. The builders felt a cold chill, wondering just what they had discovered.

The skeleton was sent away for examination and work was carried out on the remains to try and establish who it could be. The result shocked many but also solved a long-standing mystery: it was discovered that the skeleton found sealed in a coffin was that of Samuel Farrow, who had disappeared so many years ago. It is thought that after Samuel was knocked unconscious by his brother during the fight in the High Street, he was dragged upstairs. Thinking Samuel was dead, Timothy sealed him in a coffin – but Samuel was still alive. Researchers found marks on the inside of the coffin lid that had been made by Samuel's nails as he tried to claw his way out of the coffin in which he had been entombed.

There have been strange noises in the old post office over the years. Some people have heard nails being knocked into wood when no one is doing work on the property. Others have heard the scratching of fingernails on wood. However, since the skeleton was discovered, the feeling of unease has gone – it is as if Samuel was crying out to be found.

The Cinque Port Arms

The Cinque Port Arms in All Saints Street is one of around eighteen historic inns in the Old Town, all of which have fascinating stories surrounding them. At one time there were around forty inns in the old quarter but many of these disappeared in the Bourne clearances. Some pubs of yesteryear are now private houses or shops. For example, the Roebuck Inn is now Roebuck House doctors' surgery and the Kicking Donkey in Hill Street is a private house.

The inns in the Old Town have served many purposes, as well as being drinking establishments. A lot of the Old Town pubs were used as hiding places for smugglers and their goods; they were ideal places with their deep, dark cellars and entrances to tunnels connecting properties and churches all over the area. The Dolphin Inn on Rock-a-Nore was a very busy inn during the smuggling era, especially on a Sunday morning after the large boats had come ashore with all their goodies. The Dolphin was the smugglers' first port of call and became one of the most notorious pubs in the Old Town, with many reports of riotous behaviour from the drinkers and sometimes even the landlord. The Fisherman's Institute was formed in All Saints Street in 1882 to try and steer people away from the evils of drink but it is not known how much success it had. At the side of the Fisherman's Institute are some steps called Creek Steps, which in the early 1900s led to a soup kitchen that provided the poor of the Old Town with a hearty jug of soup for tuppence. Inns have long been used as meeting places. The Swan Inn at the southern end of the High Street, on the corner of Croft Road, was a very grand coaching inn which was once the centre of the community, holding many society events over the years. Sadly, the Swan took a direct hit during the Second World War and sixteen people were killed; the little garden on the site was created in memory of the victims.

With such an eventful past, it is not surprising that ghosts linger in the inns of the Old Town, including in the Cinque Port Arms. This inn is an impressive building dating back to 1824, although it was partly rebuilt after a fire wrecked much of the property in 1925. It is said that the presence of the original architect can still be felt in the old pub today, especially if there is any work being carried out on the building. The ghost appears to act as the guardian of this lovely old building, protecting the historic architecture. If work is carried out which does not meet with his approval, the old architect becomes very mischievous and the workmen's tools and other objects go missing. Puffs of pipe smoke have been seen when no one has been smoking in the building; this coincides with any work that is being carried out at the time and becomes more apparent if serious alterations are being considered. However, all has been quiet for some years now, so perhaps everything meets with the old architect's approval.

The Music Hall Singer

The Deluxe leisure centre on the edge of the Old Town was originally built as a music hall in 1897. It was called the Marine Palace of Varieties, becoming the Royal Cinema de Luxe in 1910. It is easy to imagine how this magnificent old theatre was once the centre of the Old Town; people came from all around to see singing, recitals, short plays and dancing. However, for a young lady from a wealthy background, the music hall was not the place to be seen. Doing this type of work gave out the wrong impression of your family and it was certainly frowned upon if you were a young lady who hoped to marry one day.

The Marine Palace of Varieties had one young songstress who sang under the name of Elaina. The daughter of a wealthy local family in the Old Town, Elaina led a double life. She loved her evenings singing on the stage but she knew that if her parents found out they would be very upset and would demand that stopped singing. So she had to lie to them and tell them that she was teaching students in their homes when she was in fact singing her heart out at the music hall. She always took a change of clothes with her and the minute that she was out of sight of her home she would change into the glamorous dresses and feather boa that she was known for.

Elaina thought that she had kept her secret safe. However, with the Old Town being such a small place and everyone knowing everyone else, it did not take long for the news that their daughter was singing and making an exhibition of herself at the theatre to reach her parents. They could not believe that their well-brought-up daughter could do such a thing and so they decided to go to the music hall one night to see for themselves and put an end to their daughter's scandalous lifestyle.

They took their seats among the many happy theatregoers and watched and listened in horror as their daughter appeared on the stage and sang to the crowds. They were horrified that she could bring such shame to the family name. At the end of her performance, they stood up and told the audience what a deceitful person their daughter was. They demanded that she come home with them immediately and told her that she was never to sing there again.

Poor Elaina did not want to leave the theatre, as she was never happier than when she was singing on stage. The theatre brought her alive and she wanted to stay there forever – even if it meant leaving her family and never seeing her parents again. She was so distraught that she committed suicide. She was found hanging in her dressing room with a note which read: 'I never want to leave the theatre as I am happier here than I have ever been and I never want that happiness to end'.

Elaina got her wish – her spirit has never left the building and her golden voice has often been heard by both staff and visitors. Sometimes when workmen have been in the leisure centre

A ghost galleon was often seen from a flat on Hastings seafront.

on their own, they have heard a beautiful voice singing but have not been afraid, thinking it was a radio they could hear. The ghostly figure of a young lady dressed in a wonderful dress, hat and scarf has been seen walking happily down George Street with a spring in her step before disappearing into the old theatre building. It can only be one person – Elaina.

The Ghost Galleon

Most of the ghosts that haunt Hastings can be traced to past events. However, there is one intriguing tale that cannot be explained – the story of the ghost galleon. The mysterious ship was seen by a retired lady who lived in a flat along Hastings seafront, between the pier and Warrior Square Gardens. She had moved to Hastings when her husband died; the couple had spent many a happy holiday here by the sea and so she wanted to come back and relive those moments during her retirement.

The properties along this part of the Hastings seafront are tall, elegant houses. They have been converted into flats today but would once have been individual houses. Wealthy city residents bought these huge houses to accommodate all their family and staff when they came to Hastings, often for several months at a time, to take the sea air. The old lady viewed several properties but one particular flat felt different from the others, as if it was in some way special. Although the other flats she had looked at also had excellent sea views, she felt that the view of the sea from this flat was perfect. She could not pinpoint why she fell so much in love with that flat but she knew that it was where she wanted to live.

The old lady moved in shortly afterwards, on a glorious summer's day. She had been in the flat for a month when, early one September morning, she gazed out to sea from her sitting room window and could not believe what she was seeing: anchored close to the shore was a magnificent galleon. She stood transfixed by the beauty of the ship, unable to move. She wished that her husband was there, as he had a great passion for such vessels. The galleon was there for around five minutes and then it just drifted away. The lady was fascinated and, convinced it must be part of some festival of the sea, she made several phone calls to find out about it. To her surprise, she was told that there was no festival on at that time. She was also told that the local authorities would have been informed of any large ships coming into the area. There seemed to be no rational explanation. The galleon appeared again on the following two mornings but then was not seen again for some time.

A year later, the old lady had her niece staying with her. One morning, the niece ran into her aunt's bedroom, urging her to get up and see the spectacular ship out at sea. They both looked at the galleon in wonder, as it shone like gold on the waves. The old lady was relieved that someone else had witnessed the ship, as she had been afraid that she was losing her mind. Her niece recalled reading about these ships: known as ghost galleons, they were said to appear to people who had lost someone close to them who was connected to the sea in some way. The old lady's husband had been an officer in the Navy and had spent a lot of time away at sea.

Over the years, the old lady has often caught glimpses of the ghost galleon, which is only ever visible from one particular window in her flat. She loves to see the ship, as she feels that it is her husband watching over her in some way.

Terrifying Twittens

There are passageways and twittens running all over the Old Town, joining up many quaint squares and snickleways. The main thoroughfares – the High Street, George Street, The Bourne, All Saints Street and Tackleway – are linked by a maze of interweaving passages. Their function has always been the same, to provide shortcuts for residents. Wandering along the narrow passageways, it is easy to see how the alleys provided the smugglers of Hastings with an ideal place to work. Some twittens appear to be dead ends, others double back, and some lead you to magnificent hidey-holes which you would otherwise never have found. These alleyways were also frequented by petty thieves and were not a place to linger in after dark. Many locals lost their way in the passageways at night and were robbed of their jewellery, watches and money. The thieves were rarely caught because the twittens were so dark – there were some places where even the moonlight could not penetrate – that the miscreants could not be identified by their victims.

Above and below: *The haunted passageways of the Old Town are not places to linger after dark!*

Today, these passageways still have a very creepy atmosphere if you dare to wander down them after dark. Although thankfully we now have modern street lighting, there are still some dark, eerie corners that the light never reaches, and you can never be sure whether someone, or something, is lurking there. Many say that the passageways are home to the spirits of thieves, still lying in wait for their next victims.

The Most Haunted Inn in the Old Town

The inn which deserves this grand title is the Anchor Inn in George Street. Until the seventeenth century, the sea used to come up to the bottom of the cliff and the Anchor Inn was originally built on stilts. Small vessels would be anchored to the stilts while their owners popped inside

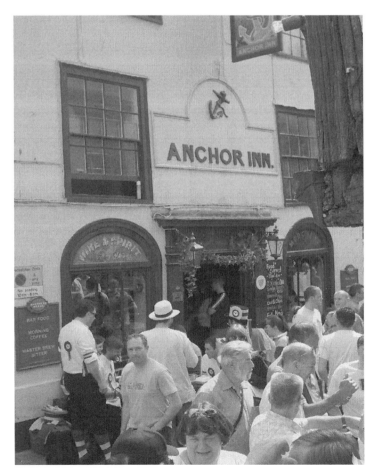

The Anchor Inn is said to be the most haunted inn in the Old Town.

the old inn for a drink, hence its name. George Street suffered from flooding right up until the 1920s, when the Bourne clearances began and sea defences were constructed. The Anchor Inn is a grand building with a great atmosphere – perhaps this is why so many spirits from the past have chosen to linger here.

Before the court and the gaol were built in Court House Street, the back bar of the Anchor Inn was used as a courtroom and many local criminals were sentenced here for crimes such as theft and unruly behaviour. This may explain why the figure of a tall man wearing a dark suit and a top hat is often seen in the back bar. There used to be a portrait of an old judge hanging in the Anchor Inn and the figure looks very much like him. It is said that the judge's spirit returns to make sure that the locals are behaving themselves.

A benevolent spirit lingers in the upstairs rooms of the inn and she has been seen by many who have stayed here over the years. Guests have reported waking in the middle of the night to see the figure of a lady wearing a big, floppy cap leaning over them. They recall feeling as if they were being tucked in and none of them has ever been afraid – they even say that they went back to sleep very quickly, as the face of the lady was very calming and reassuring. She is said to be the ghost of one of the nannies who used to work here, looking after the children of the house. One of her last tasks each night would have been to make sure that the children were sleeping and safe in their beds and it is thought that her spirit returns to watch over anyone that stays at the Anchor Inn today, to ensure that no harm comes to them.

The Anchor Inn also has a very unusual presence: the spirit of an old clockmaker who used to frequent the back bar. He was a well-known character in the Old Town and used to make and repair wonderful timepieces. Locals were saddened when he died in 1811 and he was greatly missed. His spirit is never seen or heard in the inn but he is definitely active, as broken clocks or watches left on the back bar overnight will be in perfect working order by the morning.

The Smugglers' Cottage

It is thought that in the eighteenth century, ninety-nine per cent of the population of Hastings Old Town was involved in smuggling in some way or another, and there are many tales of the smugglers' exploits. One reminder of this time is the smugglers' cottage at the top of the High Street, which would have many a tale to tell if it could speak. The cottage has a huge chimney and it is said that the smugglers would hide some of their illicit goods in this rather obvious hiding place to fool the customs guards, who would look here and think they had found the contraband when it was in fact only a fraction of the goods hidden throughout the Old Town.

There is an elaborate maze of tiny passageways and tunnels under the streets of the Old Town, linking the East and the West Hills and many of the churches, inns and houses in the quarter. These were used by the smugglers, who brought their goods ashore on the beaches and entered one of the many well-concealed tunnels, making their way to one of the many inns and their waiting customers. Once inside the tunnels, they could easily lose anyone who tried to follow them. The passages were dug out by the smugglers and the routes were handed down from generation to generation. Many customs guards were lost down the dark tunnels, as anyone unfamiliar with the passages found it almost impossible to find their way out. A lot of

The Smugglers' Cottage.

the buildings in the Old Town are built on high pavements because many of the properties have interconnecting cellars. It was very common for the inhabitants of a house to be interrupted by a smuggler emerging from their cellar to make his way out into the street to continue on his way.

The smugglers' cottage has a tiny window in its side wall, facing down the High Street. Smugglers out at sea with a boat full of gold, brandy or tea needed a reliable way of knowing if and when it was safe to come ashore with their goods, so they could avoid the patrolling customs guards. They would pay the residents of the smugglers' cottage to help them place a lantern in the tiny window if it was safe to come ashore. The smugglers would look in the direction of the cottage as they approached the coast and if there was only darkness, they would stay out to sea until the light appeared.

The residents of the Old Town are no longer involved in this illicit trade but the old cottages and inns are still populated by the ghosts of these daring smugglers and the ghosts of lost customs guards still roam the warren of tunnels under the streets.

Fishing boats and net huts on the beach.

The Jolly Old Fisherman

Hastings Fishing Beach is the heart of the old fishing quarter. The fishing industry for which this part of East Sussex is famous continues today, using a combination of ancient traditions and modern machinery and fishing methods. The fishing beach is a great place to explore, as it is possible to wander among the working boats and the net huts. There have been net huts on the beach for many centuries but the ones that can be seen today were built in the mid-nineteenth century; they are tall and narrow because of the lack of available space on this part of the beach at that time. Over the years, a lot of restoration work has been carried out on these wonderful structures by the Old Hastings Preservation Society. Many shipwrecks have been found off the coast of Hastings and it is said that the area has more shipwrecks close to land than any other county in the UK. There must be many lost souls haunting this part of the coastline.

A group of children enjoy the beach at Hastings.

Spirits and monsters lurk in the stormy seas off the coast of Hastings.

The Jolly Old Fisherman is what locals affectionately call the ghost who haunts the fishing beach. Fishermen working on their own have often looked up from their task to see an elderly fisherman with a pipe in his mouth merrily giving a helping hand with tidying or mending the nets. He is such a jolly old chap that the fishermen feel quite lonely when he hasn't been seen for several months. Some people wonder where he goes to during these absences and, as a similar spirit has been reported in Rye, it is thought that perhaps the Jolly Old Fisherman wanders up the Sussex coast from time to time to help out the fishermen there. However, he always comes back to his home – the Old Town of Hastings.

Ghosts of the Sea

Talk to any old fisherman or sailor and he is bound to be able to tell you many a tale of sea monsters and 'things' which lurk in the ice-cold waters off the coast of Hastings. Some will tell you of a nasty-looking fish that attacks boats if they do not keep to their right course. Back in smuggling times, stories of sea spirits were told to keep people on the land and to stop them venturing to where boats were laden with illicit goods. However, stories of sea spirits or ghosts are still heard today. Some people have described seeing a strange mist gather over their vessel, taking on a strange and frightening form. People have even seen this from the beaches and have alerted the coastguard, but it always vanishes by the time they arrive. No one has any real explanation as to what this strange phenomenon is but it is a very frightening presence.

Hastings Castle

Sadly, only about half of the magnificent Hastings Castle remains on the West Hill today. However, it is not hard to imagine how towering and majestic the castle must once have looked to visitors or to enemies planning an attack. The original building is thought to have been built in 1056, shortly before the Battle of Hastings, which actually took place some 5 miles north of the town of Hastings at the small market town today known as Battle. In 1216 the King feared invasion and so he ordered that Hastings Castle be dismantled. It was restored in 1225 but unfortunately the storms and natural erosion which hit the coastal town in the thirteenth century destroyed a large part of the harbour and the castle and it fell away into the sea beneath. After the harbour began to fall into decay, the town was regarded as being of little military importance and returned to its role as a fishing port. In the late sixteenth century, what remained of the castle became the property of the Pelham family and much of the ground was used for farming. The ruins became a popular tourist attraction in Victorian times and in 1951 the castle was sold to the Hastings Corporation for £3,000. Today the castle is still an attraction to visitors from all over the globe, who come to soak up the atmosphere of this ancient place.

The haunted ruins of Hastings Castle.

Many people have entered the castle over the centuries – some of them never left and their spirits still linger in the ruins. The dungeons are said to be the most haunted area. The prisoners that were kept captive here were tortured in horrific ways and many had their tongues ripped out so that they could not talk to one another. The ghostly cries of these poor souls can still be heard by those brave enough to enter the castle grounds after dark. The ghastly sounds have been known to send some people mad.

Hastings Castle is also associated with black magic, as the black witches of Hastings used the place to practise their witchcraft and to make animal sacrifices. However, there is also a romantic legend attached to the castle: it is said that if a true native of Hastings, one who was born here and has lived their whole life in the town, goes out to sea in a fishing vessel on 14 October, the anniversary of the Battle of Hastings, and looks up at the castle in the moonlight, they will see the castle as it looked many, many moons ago.

Alexandra Park

Hastings and St Leonards have several parks and gardens for the public to enjoy and the largest of these is Alexandra Park. It runs alongside an ancient stream which flows from old Roar Ghyll to the sea at Harold Place. One of the first garden areas of the park to be laid out was Shirley's Pond, created by local man Mr Shirley in the 1830s. This area can be found at the main entrance to Alexandra Park by the railway bridge and the boating lake in St Helens Road. In 1872 plans were drawn up to enlarge the park and to include local woods and a reservoir. Part of the woods date back to smuggling times and walking through them today, it is not difficult to imagine smugglers lurking among the trees.

The park was redesigned in 1878 by Robert Marnock, a well-known landscape gardener who had worked on projects such as Regent's Park Gardens. The Prince and Princess of Wales formally opened Alexandra Park on 29 June 1882 and two trees, an oak and a beech, were planted near the bandstand to mark the occasion. Since then, the park has expanded; it now runs for 2½ miles and covers 110 acres. It offers beautifully laid out rose and flower gardens, wooded walks, leisure and sporting activities and peaceful lakes and streams. Magnificent plants and trees have been planted throughout the park, offering great beauty to the area.

When darkness falls, two ghosts make their presence felt in Alexandra Park. For years, a Hastings resident used to walk his dog in the park every evening, usually at 7.30 p.m. Each night he saw the same figure, which he described as a gentleman dressed as if from another age, wearing knee-length trousers, a jacket and a hat and holding an old-fashioned lantern. Hanging from his belt was a large key and chain. The figure would walk the same round each night and end at one of the cottages near the park entrance. The figure never spoke or acknowledged the dog-walker; it was as if the gentleman was intent on finishing the task in hand. This ghostly gentleman is perhaps an old park keeper checking that all is well in Alexandra Park.

The second ghost is connected with one of the memorial benches in the park. There are many of these benches, bought to honour the memory of a deceased loved one, in the parks, gardens and other public spaces in the town. One particular bench in Alexandra Park is said to be haunted by the ghost of the gentleman to whose memory it is dedicated. A local resident walked her dogs at around the same time each evening, always walking the same route around Alexandra Park. She would start and finish at the flower garden area and invariably ended the walk with a rest on one of the memorial benches, thinking about the day's events and life in general.

One evening, she was sitting on a bench considering where to go on holiday. Her husband had died three years earlier and this was going to be her first holiday alone. She mulled over several destinations then just as she started thinking about India, where she and her husband had spent many a happy holiday, she heard a voice say, 'I'd go to India, my dear.' The voice was so clear that it was as if there was someone sitting next to her on the bench. The lady was quite shocked at hearing a voice, as she hadn't realised she had spoken out loud nor that she was sharing the bench with someone. However, as she looked round she saw that there was no one sitting next to her. She was mystified as to where the voice could have come from and put it down to her mind playing tricks on her.

For the next three days, she sat on the same bench and the voice, as if by magic, offered her advice about whatever was on her mind that day. She was intrigued by this presence and did not feel afraid at all. One night, she decided to ask the spirit who he was and the voice replied, 'I am

Two ghosts have been seen in Alexandra Park.

Colin.' She felt even more at ease now that the voice had a name. Over the next few months, the lady chatted with Colin every night and he gave her help and advice when needed. Then, as mysteriously as it began, the voice stopped. The lady felt very alone now that her friend seemed to have gone.

One night, as the lady sat on the bench, she looked at the plaque to see who the bench was dedicated to. The inscription read: 'To my dad Colin, in loving memory'. The lady wondered whether this was who she had been talking to but, thinking she would never know for sure, she decided to put it all in the back of her mind. However, the following weekend she was reading the local newspaper when one story leapt out of the pages at her. It was about some new and rare flowers that had been planted in Alexandra Park in memory of a gardener who had brought so much love and care to the park but had died suddenly. The newspaper went on to say that he was a very well-known character in the park and that these flowers were being planted opposite his memorial bench, which had been placed there around ten years ago. The lady felt a great sense of warmth when she read this story and the next day when she visited the park, sure enough some beautiful plants had been planted opposite the bench. From then on she continued to chat to her new spirit friend and formed a unique friendship, bringing together the past and present in a wonderful way.

The magnificent churchyard of All Saints' church, where treasure is still rumoured to be hidden today.

All Saints' Church

This church can be found at the top of All Saints Street and has an interesting graveyard to explore. All Saints Street has changed its name over the years, having been known at various times as Fish Street and Fisher Street because of its connections with the fishing industry of Hastings. The majority of the local fishermen and their families lived in All Saints Street and the adjoining twittens. The original All Saints' church was much nearer the sea but was vulnerable to storms and invasions. The church that can be seen today was built further inland around 1400.

There are many tales of ghosts haunting All Saints' church but one story in particular has been told for many years. In the early nineteenth century, a young priest came to the parish of All Saints. He was a young and likeable gentleman and settled in well to his new life. He hadn't been in the Old Town long when it began to be rumoured that he was helping the Hastings smugglers with their work. It was said that he was hiding gold and brandy in the churchyard and even in some of the graves. At first, these stories were dismissed as idle gossip but as time went

All Saints Street.

on the stories persisted and so the local parish decided to investigate the alleged goings-on. They lay in wait for the young priest and eventually he was caught red-handed dragging a large and awkwardly shaped sack across the graveyard late one night. He was then seen digging a hole and emptying the contents of the sack into it. It was at that point that the guards intervened. The local community was greatly shocked that the priest was involved in smuggling, especially as he was using the church for his work.

The punishment for helping smugglers with their crimes was severe and the poor priest was hanged on the beach early one morning. Public executions were seen as entertainment at that time and the hanging would have been a very public event, with people turning out with their families, their knitting and their sandwiches in tow. Before he was hanged, the priest told the town officials that they hadn't found nearly half of the gold coins that he had buried in the churchyard of All Saints'.

The priest's body was buried in an unmarked grave at the very back of All Saints'. To this day, no one has been lucky enough to find the buried treasure but the legend says that if you are brave enough to venture up to the graveyard after dark and lucky enough to see the ghost of the priest, he will lead you to where some of the gold is still buried.

Waterloo Passage, the most haunted passageway in the Old Town.

Little Molly Hawkins

Halfway up the High Street you will find the FILO (First In Last Out) public house. A sanctuary for the beer-lover, it offers many delights brewed on site. The FILO often hosts its own famous beer festivals and gives guided tours, which are a real treat. Along the side of the FILO is Waterloo Passage, said to be one of the most haunted passageways in the whole of the Old Town as it has had more reported sightings than anywhere else. Waterloo Passage was used as a link to the fishing quarter before Bourne Road was built. The Old Town used to consist of two main parts, divided by the river Bourne (now known as Bourne Road; the river still flows beneath the road and out to sea). The east part of the river was the fishing quarter, comprising All Saints Street and the adjoining streets. This was where the poorer residents lived, many of them fisherman and their families living in tiny cottages. To the west of the river, in total contrast, was the High Street and George Street. This was where you would have found merchants, doctors, banks, shops and the market. This was the wealthy part of the town. The two parts of the Old Town lived very separate lives in their own communities and seldom really mixed.

Molly Hawkins was the young daughter of a fisherman. She would often wander over to the High Street and gaze in the shop windows at the many delights on offer: the milliners, the dressmakers, the confectioners – all luxuries which her family could never afford. Molly would often sit and watch the well-dressed people go about their business, dressed in gowns of beautiful rich colours and textures, and she often dreamed that one day she and her family would be like them. She imagined taking them to have tea and cakes at one of the tea shops in George Street, but this was only a dream as it was all that she could do to find food for her father, three brothers and two sisters each day. Her mother had died in childbirth two years earlier when Molly's younger sister Emily was born. Until then, they had got by with Molly's mother taking in washing from one of the large houses, but now it was a real struggle. Molly's father was a fisherman and things were not always good.

Sometimes Molly had to steal food from the local traders so that they could eat. No one knew about this; her father would have killed her if he had known. The local traders had for some time turned a blind eye to Molly's behaviour but times were not good for them either and they decided to put a stop to the thieving and take Molly to the police, so they lay in wait for her one day. That particular day, Molly decided to pinch some apples as a real treat for her family. She managed to put four big red rosy apples in the large pockets of her ragged skirt without being seen – or so she thought. She made her way home as she always did, without a care in the world, laughing and skipping up the High Street. Halfway up the street, she stopped to look in a window and, as she did so, she heard a whistle blow and someone shout 'Stop, thief!' Molly looked round, horrified to see three guards running up the High Street towards her. She could not believe this was happening to her and she ran as fast as she could up the High Street to Waterloo Passage. She ran along this passageway, one she had run along so many times before, and set foot on the wooden bridge which crossed the river Bourne. As she set foot on the bridge, she slipped and lost her footing and fell into the cold water below. The traders who were following her saw what had happened and at any point they could have rescued Molly, but as a lesson to other children and to teach them not to steal from the traders they let her drown in the river Bourne.

Molly's spirit lingers in Waterloo Passage. You would think that hers would be an unhappy spirit but the ghost of little Molly Hawkins is quite the opposite. Many have reported seeing a young girl dressed in ragged clothes and shawl and with her hair in braids, skipping and singing along Waterloo Passage, just as she would have done many times when she was alive. Others have reported the mysterious appearance of a single apple in the passage now and again. The only explanation is that Molly is returning the apples she stole many years ago.

The Phantom Stagecoach

Number 23 High Street is a grand and imposing house. Today, it is a private residence surrounded by small shops and houses but the area behind the house was once a coaching station. A thrice-weekly stagecoach from Hastings to London was introduced in 1794. The coach left at 5 a.m. and arrived in Tunbridge Wells at 12 p.m, before continuing its journey to London. Several coaching stations cropped up around the Old Town, as well as coaching inns. The coaching

Above: *The phantom stagecoach left the coaching station at No. 23 High Street in 1796 and was never seen again.*

Opposite: *The sound of horses' hooves are often heard in the High Street on cold winter's nights.*

station at the back of No. 23 High Street would have been very busy, with coaches and horses and people and packages destined for the important ports of Dover and Folkstone, the town of Tunbridge Wells and, of course, the City of London.

In November 1796, a coach was preparing to leave the Old Town of Hastings late one night. There were some important legal documents on board and the coachman had strict instructions to go to a particular address in the city and not to stop for anyone or anything. The coach was loaded up and ready to leave Hastings when the head coachman appeared and ordered his coachmen not to set out, as there was very strange weather hanging over the Old Town and also reported in the country surrounding Hastings. He was worried that his men would be lost in the mist. People rumoured the weather was not like anything that had ever been seen before. However, the coachman whose job it was to go to London disobeyed his employer's orders and decided to head off, despite the head coachman begging him to stay in the town and set off at dawn when the weather had cleared. The head coachman did not know that his employee

had been offered a hefty bonus if he got the documents to their destination in the given time. Despite all the warnings, the coach left Hastings bound for London.

No one really knows what happened to the coachman but he was never seen again. Some think that he was set upon by highwaymen and brutally murdered, the coach and horses stolen. Others think that his mysterious disappearance was caused by that strange, thick mist that was lingering over the town that night and suggest that he was dragged away by the demons in the mist. The coachman's disappearance will always remain a mystery.

Often, on a cold winter's night, the residents of the High Street will hear horses' hooves galloping up the street. However, when they look out of the window there are no horses to be seen, only a strange, lingering mist. This is said to be the spirit of the coach that disappeared all those years ago. It is still trying to find its way back home but remains forever lost in the mist.

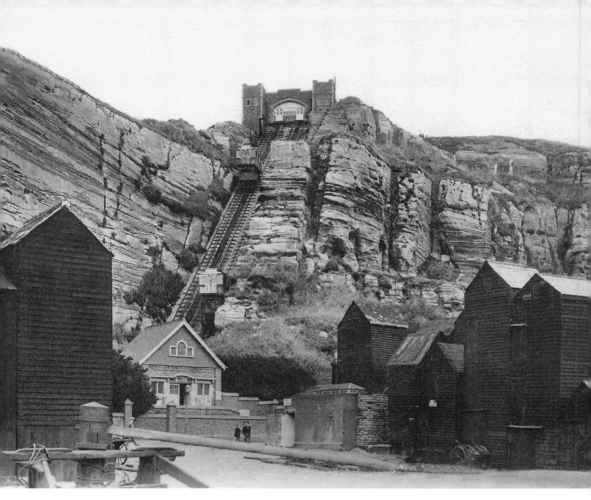

Cliff railways carry people up the East and West Hills. The West Hill railway is haunted by a mischievous orb.

The Mischievous Orb on the West Hill Cliff Railway

The East and West Hills of Hastings divide the valley in which the Old Town of Hastings so happily nestles. The West Hill is home to the Smugglers' Adventure Caves and the magnificent Hastings Castle, which looks out over the valley and the sea. The East Hill houses the Country Park and continues to Fairlight, with miles of beautiful countryside and coastline, and caves and glens ideal for those wishing to escape the noise of the modern town. Both hills can easily be accessed on foot but those wanting a more leisurely approach and the opportunity to take in some of the breathtaking views can take one of the cliff railways. The East Hill cliff railway along Rock-a-Nore road is reportedly the second steepest in this country. It was created in 1902 and is said to have been built by hand. The West Hill cliff railway dates from 1891 and runs partly through a cave.

It is the West Hill cliff railway which is said to have a very mischievous phenomenon attached to it. It has been affectionately called the Mischievous Little Orb, as that is exactly what it is. One resident of the West Hill takes the railway most days from George Street and many times has seen a wonderful ball of light just where the railway travels through the cave. Rather interestingly, it is only seen by this gentleman when he travels alone in the carriage. He also says that it follows him out at the top and has been known to scatter leaflets and tickets around in a naughty way as if it does not want the gentleman to leave. He says that he has never felt afraid when it appears but, on the contrary, feels an overwhelming sense of happiness. Perhaps the orb is the spirit of one of the construction workers who built the railway or maybe it is just a lonely little soul making friends with the locals.

A Fairy Seamstress

Fairies can be very helpful as long as you stay on the right side of them. Farmers are very often the people that they choose to help because of their work with nature. Fairies used to put silver coins in the boots of hard-working servants and they are also known for rewarding children with silver coins when they place a tooth under their pillow at night. Fairies can be found anywhere if you look hard enough but favour rural areas because of the peace and quiet they provide and also because of their friendship with nature. Sometimes you may wish for the help of fairies or just want to see them. There are many ways to summon them. If you run around a fairy ring nine times on the first night of the new moon, it is said that you will hear sounds of music and laughter coming up from the underground homes of the fairies. Fairies, however, like to work in secret and get rather upset if their work is disturbed. They love to dance, and Midsummer's Night is a very good time to see them. They also love to gather at historical places at that time of year. Fairies have been given all sorts of names over the years; in Sussex is they are frequently called pooks. This name crops up in placenames in the county, for example Pook Hill and Pooks Wood.

There is a wonderful story about the work of a fairy in the Old Town. George Street and the High Street used to be the wealthy part of Hastings Old Town and in this quarter you would have found merchants and luxurious shops, selling and making gowns, hats and jewels, to name but a few of the trades. Once such dressmaker's business was a real favourite with the young ladies of the town and the poor seamstress had many gowns on an urgent order, including one which had to be ready overnight. The poor lady worked every minute of the day, hardly stopping for a break. The dress was covered in exquisite beadwork and tiny jewels which had to be stitched one by one to the garment and the lady really did not know how she would ever finish. However, she knew that she had to complete the gown, as it was for the wife of one of the wealthiest people in the area, and if she did not finish it, her reputation as a seamstress would be ruined. At 3 a.m. the lady fell asleep, exhausted. At first light she woke with a start, terrified that she had no time left to complete the gown. However, when she opened her eyes she saw the shimmering, glittering gown hanging up, with all the work finished. She could not believe what she was seeing. She turned around just in time to see a tiny winged figure dash through a very tiny doorway in the darkest corner of the shop.

Plague Sites

The plague, or Black Death, struck Hastings, as well as the rest of the country, from 1348–50. It is said that the plague killed one in three people, resulting in 1.5 million deaths overall. There was a severe lack of any kind of medical knowledge in medieval England so no one knew how to cope with the disease. It spread rapidly and easily due to people's ignorance, poor and dirty living conditions, and limited medical knowledge. Death was very quick. Lumps appeared in the groin and armpits, followed by hideous black spots which appeared all over the body. Three days was the average time before death claimed the victims. People did not realise that dead bodies lying around waiting to be removed contributed to the spread of the disease. The methods used to dispose of the bodies were very crude and even the people directly involved in the disposal of the corpses did nothing to protect themselves against the disease and so it continued to spread.

Rats carried this fatal disease around very quickly and the Black Death had a horrendous impact on the country. Farms collapsed as workers contracted the disease and died. Industries ground to a halt. If you survived the Black Death, it was thought that you were special in some way. Many people abused this and demanded to be paid a lot more than the going rate, as they knew that the workforce was overstretched since the disease had hit so harshly and had a severe impact on workers.

People would try any cure they heard of to rid themselves of the horrific disease. One was to be put to bed and to be washed with vinegar and rosewater. Another suggestion was that the swelling be cut away, allowing the disease to run away from the body. It was also thought that applying a mixture of tree resin, flower roots and human excrement to the black spots or buboes would rid them of the shocking disease. Another extreme measure was to cut the veins from the heart, allowing the disease to escape, or placing a hen near to the swelling to draw out the evil from the body. Eventually it was realised that streets had to be kept clean of all human and animal waste. All dead bodies had to be taken to an area outside the town and burned or buried. In many villages today you will find the church is a little way from the rest of the village. Also, large plague pits were dug for mass burials of all the victims. In the Old Town of Hastings, plague pits were dug in any spare space that could be found. One is rumoured to have been dug at Coburg Place and legend says that should you linger on this site after dark, the arms of the undead will drag you down into their underworld.

Ghostly Miscreants

Courthouse Street today lies between the main Bourne Road and the High Street and has a wonderful assortment of little shops to explore. The street has led an interesting and colourful life and has seen public executions and punishments over the centuries. A medieval courthouse once stood here but sadly it was demolished in 1820 to make way for the town's gaol. The King's Head inn on the corner of Courthouse Street and The Bourne was always a popular place on execution day, as it was an ideal place to view them from. At one time, every town was issued with a pair of stocks by law. Between 1832 and 1840 the stocks in the Old Town were used solely for offences to do with drunkenness. The stocks and pillory, which were only used for petty crimes, were forms of entertainment to the locals, who would jeer and throw objects such as rotten fruit and dead animals at the poor unfortunate souls.

The King's Head is said to be home to a very mysterious spirit, whose presence is only ever felt in the ladies' toilets. People have experienced a creepy feeling when they have been in there on their own. They say that they felt as if they were being watched and they could not wait to get out. No one really knows who the spirit is but some say it is the ghost of one of the unfortunate victims who were put in the stocks. It has been suggested that the ghostly miscreant has chosen to linger here to make people feel uncomfortable, just as he felt while undergoing his public punishment.

Some people think that Hastings once had its own gibbet. Its exact location is unknown but popular belief is that it was at the top of Old London Road, on the way to Ore village as we know it today, at the crossroads near where the Sussex Arms pub is today. This would make sense, as it is outside the town and high on a hill. People were hanged and their bodies left to rot on the gibbet for weeks, as a warning to others coming into the town that this is what would happen to those who committed serious crimes. The site must have been the location of many horrific events and so it is no surprise that it is haunted. The ghost that has been reported here is a cloaked gentleman who stands very tall and straight at the crossroads, watching everyone who enters the town this way. Legend says that he will approach anyone that he does not approve of in an attempt to keep troublemakers out of the town.

Witches, Witches Everywhere

Hastings has a long history of witchcraft and sinister goings-on. Witches tried to settle in the town in its early years but were cast out. They are said to have placed a curse on the town, which resulted in the numerous invasions and battles that have taken place here over the years. The famous occultist Aleister Crowley spent time here, practising magic of various types. Black witches are said to have sacrificed animals and, some say, even humans in the castle grounds. Hastings is a magical place and still attracts a rich assortment of interesting characters.

There are many sinister tales about witches in the town. It is said that witches would lay in wait after a burial had taken place in one of the town's churchyards. They would hide among the big old trees and the dark corners of the graveyards and some say they took on the form of a large black bird if they thought that they would be seen. Once the burial was over and all the mourners were safely out of sight, the witches would reopen the grave under the cover of darkness and steal body parts to use in their spells. During the seventeenth century it was mainly only the wealthy who could afford a funeral and sometimes they were buried with their jewels on, but the witches were not interested in wealth, just the skins and bones. Many bones and other human remains were found up at the castle, where small fires would be started and magic carried out. Often the witches were disturbed and fled in fear of being caught and punished for being a witch, but they would always leave their work behind.

Not all the witches' spells were evil. Witches often worked for the good of the local people, creating medicinal preparations from natural ingredients, many if which are still used today. Over the years, people have been named as witches due to people's ignorance, sometimes just because they were ladies who lived on their own with no children and owned a cat for company.

Old Town Fires

In 1618, several disastrous fires raged through the Old Town of Hastings. Most cottages at this time were constructed from timber and had thatched roofs, so once a fire caught hold of a house it did not take long for the whole cottage to be lost to the fire. A great deal of cottages were lost at this time and, as a result, the inhabitants of the Old Town were ordered that all new houses were to be built with tile, stone or slates – no thatched roofs. The residents were also ordered to buy buckets, as it was discovered that during the fires some properties could have been saved if the inhabitants had had buckets to hand to fill with water and extinguish the flames. Many people perished in the fires, especially the sick and elderly who could not move quickly to escape the smoke and the flames. Some that survived were hideously disfigured. Many Old Town people believed that the fires were a way of finding out if you were innocent or guilty of a crime. If you survived the immense heat and flames and your scars healed quickly then you were innocent in the eyes of God and the law. At that time there was much adulterous behaviour in the town and, as a consequence, disease spread quickly through the tight-knit community – babies were even born with diseases. There were also cases of inbred families and so locals believed that these fires had been started to bring an end to this problem. Victims' screams can sometimes still be heard in the night. Whenever the sounds echo around the Old Town, the smell of burning flesh fills the air and locals are reminded of those horrific fires in 1618.

St-Mary-in-the-Castle

The magnificent St-Mary-in-the-Castle in Pelham Crescent is an architectural delight. Originally a church, it is today a popular arts centre. The 1780s saw a vast increase in visitors to the town and also the population escalated. Thomas Pelham seized the opportunity to build on his land at the foot of the cliffs to create elegant houses for the expanding local population. He decided to build a church as the centrepiece of this community. Huge amounts of cliff had to be removed before the building work could begin in 1824. Once complete, it would provide a place to worship, residential accommodation and leisure facilities, all built in a very attractive crescent overlooking the sea. The design was very striking and contemporary.

St-Mary-in-the-Castle church opened for worship in 1828, with seating for up to 1,500 people. After the Second World War, people moved away from the town centre and so attendances at the

Thatched roofs were banned in the Old Town after several fires in the seventeenth century. The victims' screams are sometimes still heard at night.

Above and oppoaite: *Pelham Crescent and St Mary-in-the-Castle.*

church began to dwindle. So much so that in the 1970s it began to be neglected. The 1980s saw the maintenance cease and the interior fell into disrepair. However, over the next twenty-five years a group of dedicated people turned the building around, raising funds and securing grants to restore this remarkable building to its former glory, and in 1997 the auditorium was once again filled with music and life.

One of the original workers on the project is said to haunt the building today. Roger Lumley was one of many locals employed to remove vast amounts of cliff before the work could begin. He was very proud of being chosen to work on such a grand project. The work was extremely dangerous and accidents and fatalities unfortunately did occur; poor Roger was crushed to death one day when the lifting mechanism failed and a huge boulder came tumbling down on top of him. Roger would often sit and smoke a woodbine on one of the many large pieces of rock, watching the sea and dreaming of foreign places. Visitors to St-Mary-in-the-Castle have often reported seeing a chap in work clothes and a peaked cap sitting on the cliff edge looking out to sea, but as soon as he is spotted, he vanishes. It is nice to think that one of the original workers still lingers to see what is going on at the site today.

The White Lady of the West Hill

There have always been unexplained phenomena on the West Hill and it is home to a distraught spirit known as the White Lady of the West Hill. In 1789 a young lady, the daughter of a wealthy family in the town, fell pregnant out of wedlock. This would bring shame and humiliation upon her family and so the young lady was sent away to be looked after by nuns until the child was born, when it would be put up for adoption. The young lady gave birth to a healthy baby boy, whom she called Alfred after the baby's father. On hearing about the birth, the girl's family ordered her to put the child in an orphanage and return home. However, she had bonded with her baby and loved him very much and was determined not to let her parents part her from him.

The girl's family arrived at the convent to take her home. On seeing her father, the girl fled from the convent, running for miles and miles to the West Hill, where she threw herself from

The figure of a lady in white has been seen running across the West Hill and vanishing over the edge of the cliff.

the edge of the cliffs with her baby in her arms. She would rather take her own life than live without her baby. The girl died but baby Alfred survived the fall because he landed on a small grass-covered ledge part of the way down the cliff face. He was taken in by the girl's family and brought up as if he was their own child. They never told him the truth about his mother.

The White Lady of the West Hill is one of the most famous ghosts in Hastings. The figure of a young girl dressed in long pale-coloured clothes and clutching a baby in her arms has often been seen running towards the edge of the cliffs and vanishing over the edge to her death.

The Phantom House on the East Hill

Many people say that there is no such thing as phantom houses, arguing that spirits can only linger on from a living soul. However, others insist that houses do have souls and can therefore haunt a place after they 'die'. Some think that 'spirit houses' are the hallucinations of the mad but there are people all over the world who firmly believe in the existence of this phenomena.

One of these phantom houses has been seen on the East Hill in Hastings. Good magic has always been practised on the East Hill, unlike the West Hill and its links with black witches and their sacrificing grounds. For centuries, the ladies of the area have come to the East Hill to collect natural ingredients for their herbal remedies and medicines. One such lady was Nelly Butter – known to many as Nelly Butterfly because so many pretty butterflies visited her garden and even followed her around – who would come to the hills and collect wild flowers and herbs for her work. She had an extensive knowledge of the natural world and her skills had been passed down through her family over the centuries. Nelly was well known in the area and people would ask her advice and seek her skills to help them with all their aches and pains. Most people trusted Nelly. However, there were those who were very doubtful of her work and thought she was an evil witch.

A wealthy family in the Old Town had a young daughter who had already tried a lot of remedies for her severe headaches. So severe was the pain that the young girl had been known to tear out her own hair to try and stop the pains. She had been to many doctors over the years but no tablet or treatment could stop the pain. Her father, who would do anything for his daughter, had heard of Nelly Butter and one day decided to take the girl to see Nelly and see if she could help her.

Nelly did all she could for the young girl but she realised that the headaches were not something that she or any doctor could really cure. She told the father that she feared that his daughter was mentally ill. The father could not accept this at all and was outraged that the old woman, who was no more than a witch, could say that his daughter was mad. If people found out that he had an insane daughter, he could lose his job and reputation in the Old Town. And so the father decided to concoct an evil and mean story and have Nelly Butterfly banished from the Old Town so that she could not practise her 'magic' any more.

Nelly's house in the Old Town was burnt down and she was sent across the East Hill and ordered never to set foot in the town again. Nelly did not mind this, as she loved the East Hill and the countryside, but she missed her friends. They helped her build a small cottage, hidden from view in a wooded coppice among all the things that she so dearly loved. Nelly did not live in her new home for very long; locals say that she died of a broken heart after being separated from her friends by the evil tongue of someone who did not want to understand her and her work. Not long after Nelly died, it was discovered that the young girl with the head pain was indeed mentally ill and a new hospital was opened on the edge of the town, where she spent the rest of her life.

Nelly's spirit still lingers on the East Hill and even though her cottage fell to the ground long ago, several people who have been out walking this way have reported seeing a wonderful little cottage, just like you would see on a chocolate box. However, when they came back to show someone else, they could not find it.

two

CENTRAL HASTINGS

The Haunted Library

Hastings Library can be found in Claremont and is also known as the Brassey Institute. The building was presented to the town in 1888 to house the library, the museum and the schools of art and science. The building has a grand feel about it, with beautiful ornate windows and a sweeping staircase which is the site of a reported haunting. A patron of the library once saw something that he could not explain. To begin with, he thought it was just the light filtering through the windows and making an odd pattern in the air but then a ball of light glided gracefully up the staircase. The gentleman watched in total disbelief, transfixed by what he was seeing. As the ball of light travelled further up the grand staircase to the top of the building, it began to change shape and the figure of a gentleman appeared. He was a wealthy, well-dressed man in his mid-thirties, wearing a suit, dress coat, gloves and a hat and carrying a walking cane in one hand. His hair was dark, glossy and well styled and he had a magnificent twisted moustache. Suddenly, the figure disappeared as mysteriously as he had appeared.

The library patron thought he must be going crazy. He had a friend who knew a little about the history of the building and so he told him what he had seen. The friend said that he must have seen the ghost that was rumoured to haunt the building, who some say is the ghost of one of the original founders of the Brassey Institute, checking that all is well in the building today.

The Town Hall Cat

The spirits of animals can appear as well as those of human beings and Hastings Town Hall has a feline ghost. The first Town Hall was built in the High Street in Hastings Old Town back in 1823; today, this building houses the Old Town Hall Museum. The present-day Town Hall was

A gentleman in black has been seen on the grand staircase at Hastings Library.

Hastings Pier. The White Rock Theatre can be seen on the left.

built in the New Town in 1881, its cornerstone being laid by the mayor of the time. It is a wonderful piece of Victorian architecture and once had magnificent chimneys, although sadly these have long gone. Down the side of the building is the Tourist Information Centre, which was once the old courtroom.

The Town Hall has a very special ghost which haunts the stairs and corridors. Over the years, many people have been involved in the upkeep and day-to-day running of the building. At one time, there was a lady who was employed as a caretaker. She used to open up the building early in the morning and lock it up in the evening. She was a popular figure who took great pride in her work and she was always accompanied by her black cat. She carried on working as caretaker until the day she died, at the age of eighty-eight. Her cat died shortly afterwards but its ghost still graces the corridors and staircase of the Town Hall. People have said that they have felt as if they were being watched and have seen a black object darting round corners and through walls. Perhaps the ghost cat is just checking that the work is being done as well as his owner did it all those years ago.

The White Rock Theatre

The impressive White Rock Theatre is situated directly opposite Hastings Pier. Many famous stars have graced the stage over the years, bringing in the crowds. The theatre was built in a colonial design; there are other examples of the architect's work along Bexhill Road. The theatre today offers an ideal venue for residents of the town and is very popular with all ages, hosting many local festivals each year, such as the Music Festival. The theatre also offers a superb bar and a café where you can gaze out to sea and watch the world go by. The site was, however, once home to a slightly less glamorous building, Hastings Infirmary, and the area known today as the Sussex Room was the old mortuary. Some people who have worked at the theatre over the years have witnessed strange phenomena but, not knowing about the building's history, have not thought much of the activities. Some events have been caught on camera. One reported spirit is a nurse who appears in the mortuary area and walks through the wall. Those who have seen her describe her as wearing long skirts and a brilliant white starched apron and cap. She is said to be carrying someone in her arms and walking in a hurry. Theatregoers think that she is an actress from the theatre on her way to the stage. Only later, when they do not see her in the show, do they begin to wonder who the figure was.

The hospital was built on this site due to the health-giving properties attributed to the sea air. However, for some patients the sight of the sea had a detrimental effect, sending them into paranoid states and trances. Perhaps this is why the building was rebuilt further inland and the site turned into a theatre full of fun and laughter.

The Ghost of Margaret Felwell

The ghost of Margaret Felwell haunts the area around Hastings Pier. The construction of the pier began in 1869 and took three years to complete. It took its design from the West Pier at Brighton. The pier offered all manner of entertainment. A shooting gallery and slot machines were added in 1910 and a bowling alley and rifle range in 1912. A paddle steamer used to make trips to Eastbourne, Rye and France and the ballroom has provided a venue for many glamorous events. The pier is one of the main attractions in the town. Just east from the pier is an underground car park and next door the sadly derelict ice rink, which closed in the 1990s. The rink used to be the public baths, called the White Rock Baths and the building dates back to 1874.

The pier, the car park and the old baths are said to be possessed by a spirit. Paranormal activity has been reported in the area, including strange electrical activity, such as lights flickering and refusing to work, and haunting screams echoing in the pier ballroom, the car park and the baths. A feeling of being watched is often experienced, as well as a sense of great unease. People have reported a strange smell, similar to that which you would find in a hospital, and dark shadows have been seen when there is nothing to cast them.

Some say that the electricity in the area has always been unreliable and that strange sounds from the sea are bound to echo around the empty spaces. However, others believe that this is

Above and opposite: *The White Rock area near Hastings Pier is one of the most haunted areas of the town.*

the ghost of an old patient from the former hospital on the site of the White Rock Theatre. The patient was Margaret Felwell from London, who came to Hastings in the hope that the sea air would cure her illness. Instead it seemed to have the opposite effect and she went insane. She had lost a baby when she was a young woman and never got over it and one night she chose to walk into the sea to her death. Her unhappy soul wanders the area, perhaps looking for her lost infant in the hope that one day the two will be reunited.

White Rock Gardens Model Village

White Rock Gardens is the second largest park in Hastings and St Leonards and dates from 1904. It offers a magnificent open space for people to enjoy, with areas of perfectly laid out lawns and flower beds to areas for sporting activities such as tennis courts and bowling greens. The Oval is a grassy area where car boot sales are held and the fairground makes its annual visit. There are plans to invest a lot into this area and make it a truly magnificent open space for all ages to enjoy.

There used to be a model village in White Rock Gardens. It was a popular attraction for

visitors but sadly had to close after the models were vandalised. Today, some of the models can still be seen as part of the putting course in the gardens. Some local residents believe that the model village was haunted. It is said that the miniature houses were inhabited by little spirits and people reported seeing smoke coming from the chimneys of cottages in the display. Lights were seen in the houses, sometimes with tiny figures silhouetted in the window and shadows in the doorways.

The Phantom Clock

The Memorial Clock Tower, built in 1861 in memory of Prince Albert, was once a prominent feature in Hastings town centre. It stood in the area which is today known as the Memorial, the pedestrianised area outside Debenhams and across to Queens Road. This magnificent Gothic clock tower was a real centrepiece in the town. Unfortunately it was vandalised in the 1970s and was demolished, much to the regret of local residents. However, ghostly ticking is often heard in the Memorial area so it appears that the spirit of the clock lives on.

The model village was said to be inhabited by tiny spirits.

Opposite: *Although the Memorial Clock Tower has been demolished, the ticking of a clock can still be heard in the Memorial area.*

Ghostly Office Workers

Today, Havelock Road is the commercial centre for Hastings, accommodating estate agents, solicitors and numerous offices. The road was developed when the railway arrived in Hastings in 1852 and Havelock Road was the main road to the station. The railway brought more business, visitors and residents to the town and much of the town centre that you see today dates back to the nineteenth century; there are some very interesting examples of architecture if you look above the shopfronts.

The University Centre Hastings on Havelock Road used to be the British Telecom building and, prior to that, the old GPO building. Over the years, BT staff on night shift witnessed strange occurrences on the top floor. There were courtesy telephones on all levels and at 3 a.m. one night, one of the telephones started to ring. No one had been seen entering the building on the CCTV security cameras. The exchange indicated which phone was ringing and so security staff went to investigate. When they got there, no one was there and nothing could be picked up on any of the cameras in place.

Staff also reported seeing a young woman walking through a vending machine – which had been placed in front of an old doorway. She is said to be Mary Frances Monk, a twenty-year-old telephonist who worked in the building during the Second World War. She was killed during an air raid, when her office took a direct hit.

three

St Leonards

Spooky Singing at Hastings College

Hastings College of Arts and Technology on Archery Road in St Leonards has always had a great reputation as a centre for education in the town and now, with the addition of the Hastings University campus in the town centre, students are offered many subjects and courses of a very high standard. The Archery Road campus has only been there since the mid–1960s and before it was built the area was a feast of architectural design. The houses around the college give some idea of what the area once looked like. St Leonards Gardens were the centrepiece of this part of St Leonards; dating back to 1830, they were opened to the public in 1880. Much of this part of St Leonards was created between 1827-37 by James Burton and further developed in the 1850s and '60s by his son Decimus. They designed it as a new seaside resort for the wealthy; it was an instant success. Highlands House was one of the grand houses of Gothic design which once graced the area. It stood on Archery Road but was knocked down to make way for the college campus. The place where it once stood is rumoured to be haunted.

Highlands House is said to have been owned at one time by a wealthy lord and lady. The lady of the house was a classical singer in London. She became sick and her husband ordered her to give up her life in London and move to the trendy resort of St Leonards, where the sea air was said to work wonders on ill people. They sold their house in the city and moved to Highlands House. The lady was forbidden to sing; she was told to rest or she would never get well again. However, she would sing in secret as she walked around St Leonards Gardens, a favourite spot of hers. Her husband suspected that she may be singing, as her illness was not getting any better, and so he decided to follow her on one of her walks. He caught her singing and told her that she had to choose between her singing or her marriage. She loved both deeply and did not want to lose either. She did not know how she could carry on living without one of her great passions. Unable to make such a difficult choice, the lady decided to take her own life. She was found by her husband one morning with an empty bottle of painkillers beside her on the bed. There was a note saying that she could not bear to live if she had to lose her singing or her husband and felt that this was the only way.

The Art Deco architecture of Highlands House.

Her beautiful voice is still heard in various parts of the college when there is no one around and also in St Leonards Gardens. A figure has been seen dancing and heard singing a beautiful song. The lady is remembered still and it is hoped that the beautiful music will carry on for many years to come.

The Masonic Hall

The Masonic Hall in St Leonards can be found behind the Royal Victoria Hotel. The hotel was built around 1828 and enlarged considerably in 1903. The original hotel entrance was situated at the back of the building so that guests could avoid the sea winds. The Masonic Hall is situated directly behind the hotel and was used as a banqueting hall. Grand balls, parties and banquets were all held here and it really was the place to be seen. Food and drinks were prepared at the hotel and brought to the hall via an underground tunnel. This area of St Leonards was part of

The Masonic Hall, where ghostly music has been heard at night.

the resort life which the Victorians in particular loved. They adored the way they could escape city and town life and come to the seaside resorts like St Leonards and be seen by others and engage in expensive pastimes. Theatres and playhouses were constructed to accommodate the visitors and their modern tastes. They brought with them elaborate clothes and parasols to keep the sun from their pale complexions. A lot of our seaside traditions were born in the Victorian era and still continue today.

The Masonic Hall was well known for its society events, none more so than the grand balls which were held there. People turned out in their finery and paraded new fashions to onlookers. Music filled the air and the atmosphere was magical. People danced and enjoyed themselves far into the night.

The atmosphere of these grand events can still be felt in the Masonic Hall. Visitors to the venue late in an evening have heard magnificent music playing, not taped music or a radio but music played by a live orchestra, even though there is no one playing any sort of music in the area. As well as hearing the echoes of the past, people have also felt an atmosphere of fun in the building, as if they had stepped back in time and were onlookers at one of the balls. Perhaps the music and atmosphere of bygone parties still lingers on for people to enjoy today.

People came to St Leonard's to enjoy themselves at the Royal Victoria Hotel and the Masonic Hall, and the atmosphere of fun lingers there today.

The Headless Smuggler of Gillmans Hill

Smuggling activity was not just limited to the shores and the Old Town of Hastings but was spread throughout the area, as much of the land was farms and woodland. The area at the bottom of Gillmans Hill, as we now know it today, was a favoured area for smugglers. It was a wooded area with good access to the coast and as such was frequented by numerous rival gangs of notorious smugglers, who fiercely guarded and protected their territories. Many stashes of illicit goods were hoarded in this area and so anyone found wandering the woods was dealt with by the smugglers.

To try and stop local people wandering into the woods and perhaps stumbling across these goods, elaborate stories were made up to frighten people. Tales of trees being possessed by the devil was a favourite, as often bags of gold and lace were hidden in tree trunks and the smugglers did not want people to find them. It was said that if people ventured too near the trees, the tree

A headless man has been seen staggering into the road at the bottom of Gillmans Hill.

devils would get hold of them and drag them away to some unthinkable place. It was also said that anyone caught looking in tree trunks for bags of gold would have their eyes gouged out so they could never show anyone where the treasure was hidden. Some locals believed these tales but others knew them to be smuggling tales created to keep people away.

Fights often broke out between the gangs of smugglers, frequently resulting in bloody battles and sometimes even death. In 1813 there was a particularly gruesome meeting between two rival smuggling gangs, one gang being from Bulverhythe and the other gang from a little way up the coast at Pevensey, who it was said were looking for new territory to hide their goods. The Bulverhythe gang did not take lightly to this invasion of 'their' woods and the Pevensey gang were set upon. It was said there were over 100 men fighting in the wooded area at the bottom of Gillmans Hill. It was a very brutal and bloody fight, resulting in many fatalities among the Pevensey smugglers. One man named Jimmy the Crab (he had been given this name due to a deformity in one of his legs, which made his walk slight abnormal) had his head cleanly sliced off. His head is said to have been placed on a pole at the entrance to the woods as a warning as to what may happen to others who venture there. The Pevensey gang admitted defeat and pulled out of the area. To this day, though, the figure of a headless man staggering into the road at the bottom of Gillmans Hill is often seen by motorists driving down the hill. It is such a shocking and worrying sight that some have got out of their cars to search for the man but he has never been found.

The Church-in-the-Wood.

The Church-in-the-Wood

The Church-in-the-Wood in Hollington, St Leonards, has long been a popular place for worship and celebrations. Legend says that there has been a chapel or church on this site since around 1080 and it is thought that the original building was constructed a few hundred yards from where it stands today. A young priest chose the location for the original church but for three consecutive nights all the building work that had been done during the day was pulled down and the priest was back to where he had started. He was mystified by this action and was told by locals that this was the work of the devil. The priest was told to build the church in the wood instead. He began building again, in an ideal spot located among the trees. Each morning he returned, expecting his work to have been undone but this was not the case and the church continued to be built. The church was called the Church-in-the-Wood as it was situated among the trees, far away from the gaze of the devil.

This wonderful little church has attracted visitors since the mid-eighteenth century. The church was lit by candles right up until 1977, when electricity was installed. The church has what is known as a devil's doorway, which was the northern entrance to the church. This would have been opened during confirmation and communion services so that the devil could be let out. One of the oldest bells in the town is housed in the bell tower of this church and is said to date from around 1371. The oldest tombstone in the graveyard dates back to 1678 but no one has any idea who is buried there.

Many spirits and orbs have been seen in this area over the years. They are always accompanied by a positive feeling and never cause any harm. In 2003, there was a wedding at the Church-in-the-Wood. Although it was a very happy day, the bride was sad that her father could not be there, as he had died a few years before. When the many photographs taken of the happy couple were developed, the bride noticed some orbs in the pictures, particularly next to her, in the place where her father would have stood had he been there. She took comfort from the fact that, on the happiest day of her life, her father was present in spirit if not in body.

The Royal East Sussex Hospital

There have been numerous hospitals dotted throughout Hastings and St Leonards over the years. Times have moved on and lots of the services they provided are now consolidated at the Conquest Hospital on the Ridge in St Leonards. Many of the old historic buildings have, since closure, been converted into private houses and flats. The Royal East Sussex Hospital was a magnificent building based in Cambridge Road, Hastings, with a vast maze of corridors, wards and offices and sweeping staircases. People walking the corridors at night, when the hospital was quiet, would feel a creepy atmosphere and there were many unexplained happenings during its long life.

There is a very sinister story of a haunted pathology lab. A doctor who trained at the hospital spent the early years of his career in the pathology lab at the hospital, identifying, researching and experimenting on body parts. Part of the laboratory where they worked was taken over by a few shelves containing jars of oddities and strange items found over the many years at the hospital. Eyes stared back at you from the jars, internal organs glistened and even parts of brains were displayed in a gory display. There was one night that the doctor will never forget. He was working on a project for his end-of-year exams and was busy dissecting an organ in the laboratory. He recalls the night as if it was yesterday. He had returned to the lab after the staff had left and all was quiet and in darkness. He was used to working at all hours on his own and quite liked the quietness of the hospital at night. He got stuck into his work but after a short while felt as if he was being watched. He kept checking over his shoulder but the only things behind him were shelves of glass jars. He worked on for another hour, conscious all the time that he felt as though someone was watching his every move. In the end he was so spooked that he packed up his work and decided he would return in the daylight. As he locked the door and started to walk out of the building he said goodnight to one of the security staff on duty and mentioned to him that he had felt as though there was some one in the room with him but could not find anyone. The security guard had also not seen or heard anyone but he did tell the doctor a story about haunted pathology lab. When the hospital was first in service there was a mad professor who taught in the laboratories. He had a very different way of teaching and was popular with his students. On his death it was his wish that his body parts be kept and displayed in the pathology lab in jars for many years for future people to enjoy. His eyes were placed in a separate jar and it is this very jar that is said to be haunted and gives the feeling that you are being watched. The professor is obviously making sure that today's students are working up to his standards.

The Wishing Tree of Summerfields Woods

Summerfields Woods has long been an enchanting and mystical place, associated with tales of fairy folk and magical trees for hundreds of years. Many stories have been passed down through the generations and are retold many times. Ancient trees have always been a source of folklore and legend. If you visit an apple tree on Christmas Day and the sun is shining gloriously on the tree then it is said that the tree will yield a magnificent crop for the following year. Celebration and worshipping of the tree spirits have long been a tradition and way of life to many rural folk in the hope that, by praying to the trees and offering gifts, the next harvest will prove very bountiful. Diviners would often use the forked branches of an apple tree in their search for water. Ash trees are often associated with evil forces and some believe that the devil lives within this tree. However, the seeds from this tree are meant to foretell your luck in love: the number of seeds your tree produces indicates how lucky you will be. The aspen tree is said to constantly shiver and quiver because it is said that Jesus Christ was crucified on a cross made from aspen wood and the tree is so distraught about this that it has sobbed ever since.

Summerfields Woods is said to have had its own magnificent wishing or spirit tree and some people think that it is still there today. No one is exactly sure which tree it is but the story goes that the tree will make itself known to you if your wish is of a positive nature. The wishing tree was very popular during Victorian times, when many believed in the existence of fairies and tree folk. A little local girl used to play around the wishing tree and talk to it as her friend and also to the fairies that lived in its branches. The little girl came from a very poor family in the area and would often tell the tree of now she longed for some pretty things. The tree approved of this wish as it was positive and not at all greedy or negative in any way and so he thought about what he could do to make the wish come true for the little girl. He did not have to think very hard at all and when the little girl awoke the following morning her small garden was filled with fruits and pretty flowers and there were bees and butterflies decorating the air. The little girl and her family were very happy, as they had never seen such wonderful things.

Bohemia House

Bohemia House in Summerfields was a magnificent farmhouse dating from 1818. It was built in a wonderful manor-house style, with an imperial-style staircase constructed from pine and wood, and vast amounts of elaborate detailing throughout the large and impressive house. The estate included a coach house which would have housed two coaches and up to six horses and also ample sleeping accommodation for the coachmen. There were mock Roman baths built to make the most of the pure natural springs in the area; these still exist in the woods today, along with an ice house. In the days before refrigerators, ice houses were packed with ice from local ponds to keep food fresh. They were constructed as a deep brick-lined well with a domed roof; sometimes they were built into banks of earth to give added insulation. Also on the estate were vast gardens, which included a private walled garden, vegetable gardens and a beautiful

Hastings Pier in the foreground and St Leonards Pier in the distance.

ornamental garden. The house was reached from the main road, where two lodges were built, North Lodge and South Lodge. South Lodge survived until 1999.

In 1903 Bohemia House became Summerfields Preparatory School for boys aged between eight and thirteen. It was a school for sixty years and many famous people were educated and prepared for life here, including the Marquis of Blandford and the King of Jordan. During the Second World War, the school was used as the Town Hall for Hastings, reverting to a school at the end of the war. It was a great loss to many people when in 1972 this historic house was pulled down, as it was a well-loved landmark in the town.

Only a stone's throw from the estate is St Paul's School. In 1979, a class from St Paul's was taken for a walk around the area where Bohemia House had been. The teacher pointed out such things as the Roman baths and the ice house. Just before they reached the site of the old manor house, one of the pupils gave her teacher an in-depth description of the great house, down to every last detail. She described how the staircase swept from the hallway, forming the centrepiece of the house. She also described the decor and elaborate design, the stags' heads hung in the great hall and the rich and elaborate drapes and colours throughout the rest of the house. She told the teacher that the ice house was only used for more luxurious foods, like ice cream, fruit and drinks, rather than everyday foods, as most people assume. The young pupil informed her teacher that she had been inside the house long ago. Perhaps this young girl had visited Bohemia House in a past life or maybe the house comes back in spirit form so that people can continue to enjoy it today and keep the history of Bohemia House alive.

St Leonards Pier.

The Phantom Pier

In 1891, the grand opening of St Leonards Pier took place. It was situated almost opposite the Royal Victoria Hotel, in an ideal position for visitors and people staying at the hotel, and became a direct rival to Hastings Pier. During the Second World War, the pier was greatly reduced in size to guard against invasion and, sadly, what was left of it was removed in 1951.

At the end of the pier was a magnificent room, used for dancing, where a local orchestra used to play the music. People visiting this area have reported hearing the sounds of a grand orchestra playing. The visitors have been very puzzled by this experience, as the music sounds as if it is coming from out at sea. This enchanting music is the ghostly sound of bygone parties and grand orchestras playing to the crowds.

Above and following two pictures: *St Leonards is haunted by the husband and the lover of a wealthy nineteenth-century lady.*

The Ghosts of Rival Lovers

The Royal Victoria Hotel on the seafront, which provided luxurious accommodation for visitors to the town, was completed in 1828. Guests often stayed for extended periods. A wealthy lady from London used stay here whenever her husband was occupied with business matters in the City, as she found herself becoming bored in a large house in London all day with only the staff for company. She would come and stay at the Royal Victoria Hotel and her husband would join her when he had completed his business. The lady spent her time by the seaside, thoroughly enjoying herself. She felt that her life was slipping away as she was now in her fifties and so she decided that she would enjoy herself. She spent copious amounts of money on drinking and partying, and flirted with any man that happened to come her way. She adored the attention that the money brought her and it didn't take long for her to develop a bit of a reputation. The hotel staff were quite used to the lady entertaining gentlemen in her room. Most of the gentlemen were a good deal younger than her, often labourers in their late twenties and early thirties who were working on construction sites around St Leonards, which caused quite a stir.

The lady's outrageous behaviour carried on for months, until her husband got wind of what was going on in his absence and decided to cut his business in the City short and travel to see his wife in St Leonards. On arriving at the Royal Victoria Hotel, the reception staff acted slightly strangely towards him. It seemed to him that they wanted to delay him in reception for some reason; thinking this was rather odd, he demanded to be shown up to his wife's room. However, he was not prepared for what he found in the room — but the staff knew only too well.

On entering the room, he found his wife with a young man. He threw the man out into the street but could not look at his wife. He loved her very much and had trusted her implicitly, and he felt betrayed and let down. That night, he decided to find the young man who was responsible for this. He had been told by staff at the hotel that the man was called James Coles, known as Jimmy, and that he could be found at the Horse and Groom pub in Mercatoria. Mercatoria was the service area for St Leonards; all the trades would have been found here and this is where the laundrywomen worked. The Horse and Groom was built for the many labourers brought to the area to working on houses in St Leonards. Around this area many houses let out rooms and provided lodgings to these young men.

The lady's husband went to the Horse and Groom and found Jimmy smoking a pipe in his usual corner, watching the world go by. Jimmy recognised the lady's husband as soon as he

The spirit of Jimmy Coles lingers at the Horse and Groom.

walked through the door and knew that he had come to see him. He left the pub, as he did not want any trouble in his local or in front of his friends. Once outside, he was confronted in a very quiet but stern manner by the lady's husband, who told him that he would never see her again. Jimmy understood and accepted the situation; he had to admit that he would miss the expensive gifts and good brandy he had been given but all good things must come to an end.

After his brief meeting with the lady's husband, Jimmy put the lady to the back of his mind. He knew that it was only a matter of time before another woman came along. Later that night, he left the Horse and Groom and began his short walk to his lodgings. However, he failed to notice the gentleman following him. He was dragged into an alleyway and his throat was cut. No one knew who had murdered Jimmy and it was blamed on the petty criminals in the area who preyed on the construction workers, knowing that they often had large amounts of cash on them.

Jimmy's lively ghost is frequently felt in the Horse and Groom today. People know that he is present if they see and smell pipe smoke coming from his favourite corner. This is a happy spirit, despite his manner of his death, and he sits and watches the world go by just as he did in life. The ghost of the lady's husband haunts the Royal Victoria Hotel. His dark shadow has been seen in the corner of one of the rooms and a couple who stayed there felt as though there was someone else in the room with them. Perhaps he is making sure that no adulterous behaviour takes place in the hotel today.

The Haunted Maze

Maze Hill, which is home to some wonderful nineteenth-century Gothic architecture and is a very interesting area to walk around, was named after the maze which used to be in nearby St Leonards Gardens. Some say the maze was haunted and there are many stories told about it. Whether the tales were made up to keep people out of the maze or whether it really was haunted will remain a mystery. The ghost of the maze is said to have taken the form of a strange wisp-like figure which would hypnotise anyone who entered the maze. The spirit would lead people to the centre of the maze then vanish, leaving its victim to find the way out alone. For some it took a long time and was a very traumatic experience. Perhaps this is why the maze is no more.

The Enchanted Windows of the Conquest Hospital

The old Buchanan Hospital in St Leonards was the maternity hospital for the area and many locals were born there (including the author and her husband). This old hospital with its winding corridors closed once the maternity services were transferred to the Conquest Hospital, a purpose-built state-of-the-art hospital on the edge of the town. Some historical artefacts were rescued, including some magnificent stained-glass windows from the chapel and other areas of

The stained-glass windows in the Conquest Hospital are said to be enchanted.

the hospital. These are now on display in certain areas of the Conquest Hospital and certainly brighten up the place. Many people say that the windows are enchanted and that they hold the spirits of long ago.

There are mentions of stained-glass windows as far back as the seventh century and by the fourteenth century, they were considered an art form. Little has changed in the manufacture of stained-glass windows, with fragments of coloured glass being held together by an intricate lead framework. In medieval times, fables were very popular and these were portrayed in many window designs. During the seventeenth and eighteenth centuries, there was a decline in this craft but the nineteenth century saw an attempt to recapture the art of the window-maker. There are many examples of stained-glass in parish churches and cathedrals today; these normally date from Victorian times.

Stained-glass windows are used to depict stories from the Bible and historical events. It is believed that many of these windows hold secret messages and they have also been used to tell enchanting tales and also to commemorate events. The different colours used also have significant meanings. The use of black meant death, blue symbolised heavenly love and the Virgin Mary, violet meant love, truth, passion or suffering and the use of white or gold meant innocence of the soul and holiness in life. The size of people or objects in the windows indicated their importance. Several symbols were used in the Christian church, including a dove, which indicated the gentle, pure and loving influence of God. If the dove was carrying a leaf in its beak, this symbolised forgiveness. Water was used to show a basic need that all life cannot live without. It is thought that the images in the windows many have been designed to educate the masses, who had little or no schooling, and to tell them the ways of the Church.

The windows that are now in the Conquest Hospital hold very positive energy and are said to be enchanted with happy spirits. Security staff on patrol late at night have reported hearing gentle singing when they pass the windows. They have also seen something move out of the corner of their eye, as if the scene in the window was moving in some way. One of the windows depicts joyful figures holding children, and the happy laughter of children has been heard by people passing this window, even though there is no one else around. The sound has been described as 'coming out of the window' and again the figures in the window seem to move. It may just be a trick of the light but many people like to think that the windows have somehow absorbed all the happiness that the Buchanan Hospital brought to local people.

The Phantom Nuns of St Margaret's Terrace

St Margaret's Terrace in central St Leonards forms part of an area rich in grand architecture dating from the late 1800s. Many properties here are of particular historical and architectural interest and fall into the boundary of the conservation area. The houses are very grand, with four or five storeys; some were built in a villa style which at the time would have been considered very modern indeed. You can see why the new resort of St Leonards attracted many people looking for a house by the sea. These imposing terraces of houses had spacious interiors, with high ceilings, bay windows and light and airy rooms. St Margaret's Terrace is only a very short walk from the sea.

This grand house in St Margaret's Terrace is still watched over by nuns.

Sea air is considered to be very healthy and some houses were turned into rest homes and care homes. One of the houses in St Margaret's Terrace became a care home which was solely for the use of nuns from the local convent. Here, elderly and sick nuns we nursed by fellow nuns. The cool, dark cellars of the house were used for laying out the dead and there were tunnels joining the convent and the care home so that bodies could be carried between the two buildings without causing alarm to local residents. Only the nuns would have known of the tunnels' existence.

The current owners of this house have witnessed some fantastic phenomena. For example, the whispering of a very gentle female voice has been heard when everyone else in the house has been asleep. The voice apparently sounded so close that it was as if someone were leaning over the bed and whispering in their ear. This could be an echo of the past when the nuns who were tending their sick would speak very gently and softly to the frailest, to make sure they were at peace.

The atmosphere in the house has a strange effect on the resident felines. They will often sit and stare at nothing, as if they are being hypnotised by some ghostly orb. Perhaps the cats are seeing the wisps that have also been visible to humans as well. The distortion of air is only seen for thirty seconds and then it is gone.

Residents at the house have also seen three female figures on several occasions, sometimes even standing around their bed. This again would link to the house's previous function as a care home, when the nuns would gather round the bed of someone sick or dying and watch and pray over them. For several months, the residents tripped up the third step from the bottom of the staircase every time they went upstairs. They say that it felt as if there was something on that step. Friends who have stayed here over the years have reported seeing a small group of women dressed in long cloaks and headdresses walking through the walls of the cellar; two of the terraced houses were one large house when it was a care home. No unease has ever been felt during these supernatural occurrences, quite the opposite in fact. The house feels very peaceful and full of positive energy.

four

WEST ST LEONARDS TO BEXHILL

The Bull Inn

At the westernmost tip of West St Leonards is the old settlement of Bulverhythe, which has a fascinating history. It dates back to Roman times, when the port of Bulverhythe existed mainly to transport iron ore from the quarry at Beauport. The name Bulverhythe means 'landing place for the people' and at one point it had its own little pier. During the thirteenth century Bulverhythe was a self-contained village mainly in the area of Galley Hill, or Gallows Head as it was known then. In the seventeenth century, Bulverhythe was the haunt of notorious smugglers – and one of their favourite places to hide goods and transact their illicit business was the Bull inn.

Ale has been served on the site of the Bull since at least the thirteenth century. Entering the Bull today feels like stepping back in time and the inn has a magical atmosphere. The ruins of the old abbey and church can be found in the back garden of the inn and stones from the ruins are said to have been used in the construction of the old inn. Many of the beams in the building came from ships wrecked off the coast. The bar area in the Bull was once used as a courtroom and many were sentenced to death here. Underneath the bar area were cells where condemned prisoners were kept before being taken across to Galley Hill and hanged at the gallows. Deep in the cellars are two passageways leading into secret tunnels. One tunnel leads south into the cliffs at Bulverhythe; it is said to have been used by the smugglers, allowing them to enter the inn undetected. The second tunnel leads north and was used by the monks, as it linked the inn and the abbey. A ghost haunts the back garden of the inn and he is thought to be a monk from the abbey who used to make frequent clandestine visits to the inn through the tunnel.

The Bull inn has connections with a famous shipwreck. In 1749 the *Amsterdam* ran aground at Bulverhythe Sands and sank. The vessel, one of the biggest ships of the time, had been en route to the East Indies, under the command of Captain Klump. Her nine-month voyage was to take her through the English Channel to the Scilly Isles, then out across the Atlantic Ocean to Batavia in Java. She was part of a fleet of five ships heading for Java carrying a total of 4.8 million guilders, mostly in silver bullion. The *Amsterdam* was carrying 300,104 guilders in twenty-four chests, which were stowed securely in the captain's cabin. There were 335 people on board the ship, including seamen, officers, soldiers and five very special passengers.

The *Amsterdam* set sail on 8 January 1749 but ran into trouble less than three weeks later when she was hit by severe storms. On 26 January 1749 she sank off the coast at Bulverhythe. Conditions on board the ship were cramped and unsanitary and diseases such as malaria, dysentery and leprosy were rife. Many had died during the first two weeks of the voyage and their bodies were removed from the wreck and buried in a small cemetery next to the Bull inn. Those who were sick were taken to a farm in the Filsham Valley. The Bull was used as a base by the investigators from the shipping company.

The *Amsterdam* sank 14ft into the sands in just one month and the wreck was not rediscovered until the 1960s. Explorations had been made into the sands in 1837, in an attempt to find the wreckage, but they had had no success. In 1969 civil engineers were working at Bulverhythe on the 150-year-old sewer which desperately needed replacing. It was at this time that the same severe weather conditions which had run the *Amsterdam* aground made work on the sewers too dangerous. Much of the work was ripped up by the 60mph winds and divers had to be brought into assess the damage. It was then that the remarkable discovery of the *Amsterdam* was made. An intense mixture of clay and quick sand made excavation very difficult but as work proceeded many treasures were unearthed, including corked bottles of wine, kitchen implements, candlesticks and hair combs. A cannon was among the items uncovered but the lifting machinery could not hold it and it was dropped into the sands. Unfortunately no record was kept of the objects removed from the ship. Work has carried on over the years and there are plans to one day fully excavate the wreck.

Looters stole some of the treasures from the ship, including bottles of wine. However, one of the bottles gave the thief more than a hangover. It is said that the bottle was possessed with an evil spirit and, when it was opened, the spirit flew out of the bottle and into the thief, sending him insane. The thief threw the bottle back into the sands at Bulverhythe from where he had stolen it. There are many spirits haunting the wreck of the *Amsterdam* and the ship's bell has been heard ringing near the site of the shipwreck on stormy winter's nights.

A Ghostly Army at Glyne Gap

At one time St Leonards and Bexhill were two distinct towns, with only the odd alehouse and farmhouses scattered in between. Today there is not much dividing the two towns except for an area known as Glyne Gap. This is an area of natural beauty with the reed bed nature reserve and the Filsham Valley area attracting many kinds of wildlife. Glyne Gap plays host to many events, including a circus which comes to town in the summer months and weekly Sunday car boot sales. The Glyne Gap/Ravenside retail and leisure park houses many High Street stores, as well as a bowling complex and a swimming pool. The fields at Glyne Gap have for some time been an area of mystery and there have been many reports of strange sea mists in this area when the rest of the town is clear.

Mr Brown, a resident of St Leonards, once had a fascinating experience at Glyne Gap. He worked on the outskirts of Bexhill and walked to work most mornings. One autumn morning in 1993 he had a walk to work that he would never forget. He started work at 7 a.m. and usually reached Glyne Gap at around 6.40 a.m. That morning, the sky was still dark, the streets were quiet and people were just starting to wake up. Mr Brown followed the curve of Bexhill Road, with the fields of Glyne Gap on his right. Something made him look up and what he saw stopped him in his tracks. A group of six or seven men were marching across the fields. Their dress was very old-fashioned, not the modern styles of today, and they were wearing body armour with face shields and carrying weapons of some sort. They seemed to have a very determined manner about them, as if they knew where they were heading. Mr Brown was glued to the spot, not sure what to think. The group marched over the fields and then, as quickly as they had appeared, they disappeared into the morning mist and were gone. These mysterious figures could have been the ghosts of soldiers going to some bygone battle, perhaps even the Battle of Hastings in 1066, or maybe they were smugglers preparing to confront a rival gang. Mr Brown always hoped that one day he would see the soldiers again, and he looked out for them on his walk to work every day until his retirement in 1998, but the magical sight never reappeared. Mr Brown died in 2001 but his wife often walks this way, hoping to see the extraordinary phenomenon for herself.

The Battle of Sidley Green

The town of Bexhill-on-Sea is a tranquil seaside town which was developed by the seventh Earl De La Warr in 1883. He succeeded in his desires to make a new and fashionable resort to be enjoyed by many. Today, Bexhill is a favoured retirement town, offering a far more sedate lifestyle than its lively neighbours Hastings and St Leonards. Looking at the grand Victorian and Edwardian architecture, it is hard to imagine that at one time this delightful town had no more than 500 residents.

In May 1902 the first automobile race in Britain was held in Bexhill. Thousands of people flocked to the town to witness this event. Vehicles raced at 50 mph along the seafront – which caused quite a stir as the usual speed at that time was 12mph. It was a glamorous event with over 200 entries in the races, and the hotels were packed. This was the beginning of what has become an annual motoring event loved and attended by many. Another daring milestone in 1902 was the opening of one of the first mixed bathing areas along Bexhill promenade. The famous De La Warr Pavilion, now a thriving arts centre, was built in 1935.

On the edge of Bexhill is an area known as Sidley, an area which has a rich history. The New Inn in Sidley was a favourite haunt of smugglers; it dates back to the 1700s, when it was known as the Eight Bells. Sidley was the site of the Battle of Sidley Green in 1828, when a gang of local smugglers came up against the coastal blockade guards. A local resident has often seen the battle taking place on the green; the scenes are so vivid that at first he thought it was actually a historical re-enactment. He has witnessed the fighting at various times over the years, always in the evening when it is very dark and the air is still. Out of thin air, the coastal blockade guards and smugglers appear and fight for some time, with some of them being fatally wounded. After a while, the ghostly figures fade away into the night air.

Bexhill Old Town

If you walk up the hill from the seafront, you will find the Old Town of Bexhill. This part of the town is quite different from the grand style of the buildings on the seafront. The buildings here mostly date back to the eighteenth and nineteenth centuries and some of the façades hide medieval structures. St Peter's church is the centre of the Old Town and is a wonderful example of Saxon workmanship with some Norman influence in the shape of its tower. Near the church is the Bell Hotel, which is thought to date back to the seventeenth century.

There are many grand houses in this area. Two hundred years ago they were home to large families who employed lots of staff, including drivers, nannies, maids and cooks. A strange phenomenon has been experienced in the area: the delicious smell of home cooking often pervades the air. Even motorists have commented on the scrumptious smells as they pass through the Old Town. Perhaps it is the ghostly echo of the many meals lovingly prepared by the cooks who once worked in these houses.

The Manor Barn Costume Museum

A stone's throw from the Old Town is the Manor Barn Costume Museum. The ruins of the thirteenth-century manor house can be seen in the gardens of the museum, as well as a nineteenth-century coach house. The costume museum houses clothes and lace from different eras and also a display of dolls. It is said that several pieces of clothing are haunted by their previous owners, as items have been known to vanish for a night and then return the next day. Some people assume that the clothes are being mended or have been loaned elsewhere but others believe that the ghost of whoever once owned the outfit borrows it for a night to wear to some ghostly event.

Bexhill Museum

Bexhill Museum, in Egerton Park, was opened in 1914 by a group of enthusiasts who were interested in natural history and architecture. A student researching life in Victorian Bexhill for a college project visited the museum one weekday afternoon, when the museum was quiet. In fact she seemed to be the only visitor that day. Not long after she arrived, she heard a gentleman's voice saying, 'If you would like to follow me, we will begin the tour.' She was very surprised at this as no one had told her about a guided tour. The student spent the next hour listening to fascinating accounts of life in old Bexhill, things which she had never heard before. The guide talked about the past as if it were the present day and the tour was all done in a very interesting and informative way. The student was pleased as she now had more than enough material for her project. At the end of the tour, she shook hands with the tour guide and he left. On her way out, the student wanted to let the other staff know that she has greatly enjoyed the tour and so approached the member of staff working there and told her about how impressed she was with the gentleman guide. The member of staff's reply was very intriguing indeed: she told the student that there were no guides there that day and that she was the only member of staff in the museum. The student was left mystified. Perhaps the guide was the ghost of one of the founders of the museum, who loved his work so much that he has never left.

five

SURROUNDING VILLAGES

The Fairies of Fairlight

Fairlight, near Hastings, has been known by various names over the years, including Pharos Lit, meaning 'lighthouse'. The name Fairlight may also be a corruption of words meaning 'bracken clearing'. The country park at Fairlight covers 5 miles of wonderful rural splendour and is an ideal place to walk, with glens and fantastic bays. This area is also known as the Firehills, possibly because of the bracken fires in the summer months or because of the huge fires which were kept alight here to guide ships safely ashore.

Over the years there have been many reported sightings of 'tiny people' who stand not more than 8–12in tall with small wings on their backs. They have appeared to many people, often watching humans working or picnicking with their families. They approach the humans with little or no fear whatsoever. Many fairy tales were told by shepherds and farmers were often said to have been helped by the fairies. Fairies also rewarded people who worked hard on the land and were kind to nature by leaving silver coins in their boots during the night. Fairies like to spend their time in peaceful places surrounded by beautiful natural surroundings; perhaps that is why they are so frequently seen at Fairlight.

Creepy Church bells

There are numerous small villages scattered over the nine miles between the towns of Hastings and Rye, together with marshland and farmland. Today, the landscape is beautiful but a few hundred years ago this place was a very eerie and daunting place to venture after dark or on a foggy day. People were rumoured to have been lost for days, wandering around the bleak marshland. Bearing in mind the lack of street lighting back then and the lack of vehicles to light up the road, it is easy to imagine what a spooky place this must have been, especially in the dead of night.

The area was frequented by smugglers and highwaymen. Smugglers would hide their illicit goods in the marshland area, knowing that no ordinary folk would wander around in the darkness of the night. Highwaymen would lie in wait for their victims; this area was notorious for such attacks.

It is not surprising that all kinds of spirits lurk in this area. One unexplained phenomenon is the muffled sound of church bells ringing. This haunting sound echoes on various nights in the depths of winter. There is no church for miles around the place where the bells have been heard so no one knows how church bells can be heard ringing in the middle of the marshes. Some do not believe the tale at all, saying that it is the beating of the heart of whoever hears them. However, others say that a ghost church haunts the marshes, perhaps one of the many churches attacked by the French and left in ruins.

Gargoyles at Pett

Four miles outside Hastings you will find the village of Pett. Today, Pett consists of residential properties and at Pett Level there is a wonderful haven for many types of birds and other wildlife. Pett Level is a great place to explore and when the tide is out you can see parts of an ancient forest that once stood here.

The church of St Mary and Peter was built in the 1860s and is well known for its large gargoyles that stare down at visitors. Many people say that the gargoyles come alive after dark and follow people home. If the victims realise they are being followed, the gargoyle turns into the devil himself. This sight is said to be so evil that the victims are severely shocked and drop down dead on the spot.

The legend surrounding these gargoyles is that when the church was built in the 1860s many designs of gargoyle were submitted but the Church did not approve of some of them, being a little too modern in taste or controversial in design. One gentleman who submitted a design was Herbert Orate. He was known for dabbling in the occult and so his gargoyles were not chosen to guard the house of God. It is said that he took great insult that his work was not chosen and decided to curse the gargoyles which were used, as his revenge on the community. The curse was broken when Herbert died in 1878 but his presence still lingers on and, looking up at the gargoyles today, you can never be too sure what they are thinking.

Wisps at Winchelsea

The ancient town of Winchelsea lies approximately 2 miles south of Rye, along the A259 from Hastings to Rye. Wandering around the quaint streets of the town, you really do get a feel for the past as you explore the little shops and inns and the wonderful churchyard. There have been up to fifty inns and taverns in old Winchelsea over the centuries and the town's fishermen and seamen have played a very colourful part in the smuggling history of Winchelsea. The town has taken a battering over the centuries: the French invaded in the fourteenth and fifteenth centuries and the Black Death hit the town hard in 1348. Many people believe that there was a plague pit on the edge of the town, where the victims of the Black Death were buried.

Opposite St Thomas' church is the Great Hall, which is said to be one of the oldest buildings in the town. Part of this building used to serve as the town gaol. Perhaps its past has something to do with the wisps and strange mists that have been reported over the years, long greyish-white wisps of light, hovering in mid-air. These have been seen around the area of the Great Hall, in the grounds and also in the graveyard of St Thomas's. Some say the wisps are the souls of the prisoners who died in the gaol.

The Lonely Monk

There were once several monasteries in the area of Hastings, Winchelsea and Rye. The Cinque Ports Pottery in the ancient citadel of Rye was an Augustinian friary in 1397 and there is still an atmosphere of calm in the building. Another monastery was at Winchelsea, high on the hill overlooking the town.

The ghostly figure of a monk has been seen by many people driving across the marshes from Rye to Hastings. The figure is said to be dressed in a brown habit, and walks very slowly along the main road with his back to the oncoming traffic, with his head bent low. Motorists see him quite suddenly and are shocked by the sight. Some look back – but then wish they hadn't because the figure has vanished. Some drivers have slowed their cars down so that they are alongside the monk, only to be very frightened when he turns their way and no face is seen in the habit.

No one knows who he is or why he is walking away from Rye and Winchelsea rather than towards them. Some say that he is an outcast monk who gave into the temptation of passion and was expelled from the monastery. His penance us to walk and walk and never stop, aimlessly wandering the bleak countryside until the end of time.

Victims of the Black Death

The village of Westfield lies 4 miles north of Hastings. It is mentioned in the Domesday Book as Westwelle and at that time the area is said to have been used for trial by water. This was a method of finding out whether someone was innocent or guilty of a crime. It is said that the pit in Westfield would have been filled with water and the accused thrown in, often with their arms tied behind their backs. Those who sank were considered innocent but would, of course, drown. A variation of the trial by water was to plunge the accused's arm into boiling water. Those who did not develop any blisters were declared innocent.

St John's church stands at the southern end of Westfield; its door is made of oak and is dated 1542. The church was originally built by the Saxons and the Normans added to it. The churchyard is situated some way from the centre of the ancient village. This is because many plague victims were buried there and the community moved away from the site for fear of contracting the Black Death from the corpses which at one point were piled high in the churchyard. There are said to be secret tunnels, dug by local smugglers, leading from the churchyard into Hastings. Many smugglers used places such as graveyards to hide their goods, knowing that their booty would be safe as not many people would be wandering around unless they had good reason.

Westfield churchyard is haunted by two young victims of the Black Death from 1348. A young girl and boy looking ill and sad have been seen in the churchyard, dressed in old-fashioned, scruffy clothes. People visiting the graveyard say that they feel as if they are being watched. When they turn, they see the ghostly figures of the two children. The figures fade into thin air but the feeling of being watched remains. Maybe these ghostly figures are guarding some hidden treasure left by the smugglers.

St Helen's Hospital, Ore

St Helen's Hospital once stood in Frederick Road, Ore. The site is now occupied by smart private residences that give no indication of what used to stand there. The hospital was a bleak place and had a very uneasy atmosphere. The original building was built as a workhouse in the 1830s and it became a hospital in the 1860s.

There are many tales told about St Helen's Hospital. It is said that petty criminals were often sent to the workhouse and treated for insanity – and most never left. There are haunting tales of staff torturing the mentally ill by making them wear heavy metal cages on their heads to try and kill the evil in their minds.

With such a harrowing history, there were doubtless many unhappy spirits roaming the building. One of the most frightening areas of St Helen's was an underground tunnel which linked two parts of the hospital. Nursing staff feared using the tunnel, as they always felt as if they were not alone. It was as if there was someone or something following close behind them. The lighting in the tunnel was always failing to work and even the workmen dreaded getting a call about this job and would insist on working in pairs.

Other local titles published by The History Press

Hastings Revisited

SUSAN E. KING

This pictorial history traces some of the developments that have taken place in the fishing community of Hastings from the late nineteenth century up to the Second World War. Illustrated with over 200 pictures, mostly drawn from the archives of Hastings Central Library, this volume highlights some of the important events that have occurred in the town, from the growth of tourism to the amalgamation of Hastings and St Leonards.

0 7524 3543 4

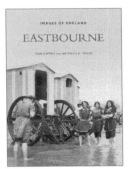

Eastbourne

JOHN SURTEES AND NICK TAYLOR

This charming collection of over 240 photographs documents life in this thriving seaside town in the late nineteenth and twentieth centuries. All aspects of everyday life are recorded here, from shops, schools and hospitals to sport, entertainment and the war years. Landmarks such as Eastbourne Pier, the Wish Tower and Beachy Head are featured and events such as the moving of the Belle Tout lighthouse in 1999 recalled.

0 7524 3682 1

Bexhill-on-Sea: The Second Selection

JULIAN PORTER

This fascinating second selection of old photographs from the collection of Bexhill Museum provides a glimpse of life in Bexhill during the late nineteenth and twentieth centuries. This collection of over 230 archive images includes Bexhill street scenes and seafront, the Old Town, Sidley and Little Common. Key events are recalled, including the opening of the Town Hall in 1895 and Britain's first motor car races on the seafront.

0 7524 2627 3

Voices of Kent and East Sussex Hop Pickers

HILARY HEFFERNAN

Right up to the late 1950s, the annual hop-picking season provided a welcome escape for thousands of families who lived and worked in the poorer parts of London, who would migrate every year to the hop gardens of Kent and Sussex to pick the harvest. The photographs and reminiscences in this book tell a fascinating story; of hardship, adventures, mishaps, misfortune and laughter experienced during hardworking holidays among the bines.

0 7524 3240 0

If you are interested in purchasing other books published by The History Press, or in case you have difficulty finding any of our books in your local bookshop, you can also place orders directly through our website

www.thehistorypress.co.uk